Beyond Graduation

by Denny Rydberg

Zondervan Publishing House

Grand Rapids, Michigan

DEDICATION

To My Wife and My Best Friend,
Marilyn

ACKNOWLEDGMENTS
I want to thank my family: Marilyn, Heather, Josh, Jeremy and Jon.
For their time and their thoughts. I also want to thank those who
shared their lives in these pages: Bruce Bailey, Bob Beschel, Phil
Harmon, Susan Hutchison, Keith Olson, Mark and Ruth Senter, Dave
Tyner, Mary Walker, Dolphus and Rosie Weary. And I'm indebted to
my team in University Ministries who critiqued my thoughts and
added their own: Gay Bailey, Steve Call, Rod Handley, Stu Harris,
Lisa Kragerud, Renee Nelson, Dave Parker, Marti Shefveland and
Laura Swain. And, finally, to my friends at Zondervan. Thanks.

Beyond Graduation
by Denny Rydberg

Published by the Zondervan Publishing House,
1415 Lake Drive, S.E., Grand Rapids, Michigan 49506.
Copyright © 1988 by Denny Rydberg

ISBN 0-310-35361-0

Edited by Shelley Hudson
Designed by The Church Art Works
Printed in the United States of America

88 89 90 91 92 93 94 95 / DP / 10 9 8 7 6 5 4 3 2 1

Table of Contents

PART ONE

A TIME FOR REFLECTION

1

Congratulations! You've commenced

On the night my high-school career officially ended, I marched down the aisle to the strains of "Pomp and Circumstance." Later that evening I gave a speech and still later received my diploma. The school officially called what happened, "Commencement." My classmates and I called it "Graduation." Whatever that time was called, it was the end. And it was the beginning.

I would no longer, as a senior, walk down the halls of good old Anacortes High. I would never again have to eat the lunches at the cafeteria. I wouldn't suit up in the colors of purple and white and charge out of the locker room while the pep band played the fight song. I would never participate in another school play, take another test, or ever again visit the principal's office. I was done. It was time to move on.

And that time for me was both sour and sweet. I was ready to leave. To become more of an adult. But I was also sorry. My high-school career had been fulfilling. I had gone to a small school where you could participate in as much as you wanted. And I had done just that. I had lived in what was then a basketball-crazed town, and I had started on the varsity for two years. The high-school teams got all the coverage in the sports section of the town's local newspaper, much as a college or pro team would get in a big city paper. So my teammates and I were well covered — semi-famous in a town of 8,100 people. When I graduated, I knew those days of pictures and articles in the paper were over.

I had grown up in a loving, supporting family. I had my disagreements with Dad and Mom. Some were major, some were not. But it wasn't a war zone. My dad was the junior-high principal when I was growing up (which complicated my junior-high years a bit) but he also had the key to a great gym, and my buddies and I played a lot of ball in fine conditions whenever we wanted. I had access to an old car in high school. I had coaches and teachers who genuinely liked me and I, them. Classes were not overwhelming, and I got solid grades. I had a girlfriend my senior year (after being afraid to date until then), and life was generally good.

But as I left the halls of the school after turning in my cap and gown, I knew that chapter was over. I didn't think about it much that evening but in the years since, I have.

The two words "commencement" and "graduation" have different meanings, as you probably know. One signals beginning or starting up. That's commence-

ment. The other indicates you've finished the race, you've run the course. You're done. That's graduation. On the night in June (or whenever you marched with your classmates and received your diploma), you did both. You graduated and you commenced.

Congratulations. You've finished high school, and you're about to embark on a whole new life. It's as if you are writing a very significant, lengthy book. You've divided the book into sections with a number of chapters in each. What you've done so far is a finished section. You've concluded a series of

When those new doors open, you are thrust over a threshold beyond which lies an abundance of pathways.

chapters in your life and are about to begin another section. The new chapter is beginning.

But maybe you don't feel like congratulations are in order. You feel totally unprepared for the next step. Or maybe you feel somewhat prepared but reluctant to take the next step.

Of course, every graduate has a different story. Some of you, like me, come from happy families and secure homes. The last eighteen years have been filled primarily with positive memories. Home was a haven. No matter how you were treated in school by friends, by a coach, by a teacher, by a school counselor, you knew at home you were loved, accepted, and important.

But some of you come from unhappy families. A tension-filled home. Your time with your brothers and sisters and parents was difficult at best. Destructive, too. You've experienced indifference, rejection, and maybe even emotional abuse.

And some come from "medium

families." Good times sometimes. Tense times at others.

But no matter what kind of family life you've experienced, most students have, before graduation, traveled a fairly defined path. Your place of residence, the schools you attended, many of your acquaintances were largely determined by your parents or guardians. Some decisions were obviously made by you, and they were significant, like "Should I succumb to peer pressure and give in to this temptation or not?" or "Who do I want to call my friends?" But many of the other decisions were already made. You knew where you would be each September (in school!). For the most part you did not have to worry about bills or cooking meals.

But at commencement or graduation, new doors crashed open. I remember the night I graduated. My parents had made it known that I was now an adult. I would no longer have a curfew. I had to make decisions for myself. That sounded great! I was ready! But I also knew that as an adult, I would be responsible for paying my college tuition (my parents helped some), making decisions regarding classes, finding a job and supporting myself.

When those new doors open, the graduate is thrust over a threshold beyond which lies an abundance of pathways. Maybe you've asked the question "What am I going to do with my life?" many times before — but now you have to answer it. Before commencement, you wondered whether you should attend college, which college to attend, whether to get a job, and which one. But now you have to act. And that can be difficult.

Graduation and the years following can be a very disillusioning time. All of a sudden the school jock, the valedictorian, the student body officer, the average Joe or Jo Anne are thrown into a new pond where past performance and honors don't make a lot of difference. Everyone is starting over. That can be good. That can be hard.

Significant honors from high

school don't carry much weight in a university of 30,000 students or even one of 3,000 or 300. An employer might look at your resume but when crunch time comes, he/she won't be looking at which school play you starred in but whether you can provide eight hours of production.

Other stretching experiences following commencement include living away from home for the first time. Sure, you've lived away from home during summers and holidays, but now you really are away. For some that may feel liberating. For others, it's a very insecure time.

It can force the question "Who am I?" when nobody knows you in the dorm and few people seem to care. Being away from home forces you to find a group, a new "home" and that can be extremely hard.

For many college students the first year out of high school may be filled with many rash decisions in an attempt to fit in. Some students begin drinking for the first time or increase their drinking. Some become sexually active. Some become introverts or "studyholics" and spend all their time in the books. Some students become

The Class of '83 left a flagpole. The Class of '84 left a bank of trees. And our class, the respectable Class of '85, would like to just *leave*.

social butterflies, running from one social event to another. Others gain the dreaded "Freshman Ten" — ten pounds of additional weight, or else they may lose weight. Some students may even develop eating disorders.

I asked a friend of mine, Gay Bailey, to describe some of the anxieties she faced when she graduated from high school and what she has seen others face. Here's what she wrote:

- There is a sense that you're standing at the edge of a cliff and you have to jump, but it feels like you're jumping into the dark.
- There is a sense of unpreparedness — "What am I supposed to do with my life NOW?"
- There is the temptation to make easy decisions if circumstances allow, just to make a decision and get on with it.
- There is the fear of making wrong choices.
- There is the thought that if you take the dumb job you are offered, you'll end up in that dumb job the rest of your life.
- There is the sense of "loss of socialization" as you leave the friends you've had for so long.
- There is the discomfort of interacting more with adults. Adults may have been, up to this point, incidental in your life, but now they've become your work companions.

- There is the depression that often accompanies change.

All of these negative feelings are well founded. As a graduate, you're on the edge — you're *required* to jump. Most likely school has not prepared you for this step. You may make wrong decisions, and they may be painful. Some people do get dumb jobs. Abrupt separation from a peer group (the crowd from high school) is a loss. It will be difficult relating to some adults. Change does produce stress. That's the downside. But it's important to know that negative feelings are par for the course at this time. It's important to know you will survive if you stick it out and take one step at a time.

Graduation can be a very freeing time too. I know of a girl who had been labeled the serious book-worm in high school. She was considered shy, but nice. When she arrived at college where hardly anyone knew her, she was freed to become the person she wanted to be. She no longer felt stereotyped. She still studied hard, but her college friends recognized her as someone who was friendly, funny, and even lighthearted. For her, college was liberating, not oppressive. Graduation from high school was a time to step out of a box she had been placed in and where she no longer wanted to live.

For me, graduation was the next step in the adventure of living. I worked at home that summer and enjoyed my newfound freedom of no curfew. I headed for college and remember the mixture of excitement and fear as I unloaded my folks' station wagon of my earthly possessions and moved them into the dorm. But I also remember the settled feeling that began to come, and I became more accustomed to my new home. Confidence began to grow. I survived. In fact, I did more than survive. I enjoyed the experience and was ready to face, four years later, the graduation/commence-ment syndrome once again.

And that's why I've written this book with some of my friends. We believe in you. We know you are special, created by God with a great life ahead of you. We want to help prepare you for your journey. We want to help instill confidence in you. We want to help you over-come any fears you may have. We want you to be freed up to face the future. We want you to be equipped, to feel like you have a good understanding of what's happening and of what you'll face, and to have a sense that you have the tools for the long haul.

But before we begin the next chapter, let me give you some words of wisdom and comfort you can apply to your life right now.

1. **It's okay not to have your**

life figured out and packaged.
Just because you enrolled in pre-engineering for your freshman year does not mean you are tied to that decision. The vast majority of students change their majors. Some, many times! Be open to new opportunities. This is a time in your life to experiment with different courses and experiences, to add depth and breadth to your life. Don't get upset or confused if you change your mind on "what I want to be when I grow up." You may even emerge from college four years later still unsure. That's okay. The key thing to remember is God loves you and offers a wonderful plan for your life. Part of the fun is being in partnership with God and discovering the abundant life with him.

2. **Choose your friends carefully.** Ask the question: what kind of people do I want to influence

me and what kind do I want to influence? The friendship factor is a big one in college. Choose carefully and well.

3. **Give priority to your spiritual growth.** Look for a fellowship group immediately wherever your new "home" is and become involved as soon as you find one. A group won't become your own until you're willing to commit time and energy to it. You probably enjoyed the benefits of a church group or Young Life or Campus Life group in high school. Don't neglect Christian fellowship in your new location. Ask your old group leader from high school to recommend or help you find a new group wherever you happen to be. A fellowship group will help provide a stable support base as you move forward. The group will also broaden your horizons as you meet and are challenged by other Christian students from a variety of backgrounds. You'll discover the Body of Christ is much bigger and wider than you ever imagined. So choose a group that will not only support and build you but will also equip you to be influential in the lives of students who don't yet know Christ.

With those three thoughts in mind, let's move on. Let's talk about one of the most important attributes you'll need as you commence. Confidence.

13

Robert P. Beschel, Jr.

Robert P. Beschel, Jr., recently received his Ph.D. in Government (with an emphasis in International Relations and American Foreign Policy). He has worked as an analyst and consultant for the U.S. Department of Defense and as Coordinator for Harvard's Avoiding Nuclear Project. He is a graduate of Ferris High School (Spokane, Washington), the University of Washington, and Harvard University (M.A. and Ph.D.).

WHAT I'D

God has been very gracious to me, and at this point in my life I have few major regrets. Looking back over the dozen years since I graduated from high school, I think there were some choices I made that were helpful and some choices I made that weren't.

First, by far the best decision I ever made was to get involved in a ministry immediately after I went to college. I worked for five years with Young Life as a volunteer leader. The spiritual discipline this fostered was invaluable. I learned what it meant to be dedicated and to put God first in the face of time constraints. I made close friendships that have endured despite years apart, and I witnessed God at work in ways that amaze me to this day. Young Life demanded a lot in terms of commitment. Yet the opportunities it provided, and the love and accountability that I gained through it, were absolutely crucial in furthering my growth in Christ. And the fact that it was a fellowship with a purpose — winning high-school kids to Jesus Christ — was extremely important in providing my faith with an outward focus.

However, I've also come to believe that it is not important for e to chart the course of my life erfectly. What is important is that am faithful where God has laced me — that I work hard, ve God, and make the best ecisions I can based upon what I now at each step along the way. have tried to do this. And I have ade some minor missteps, but ery few major ones (and those re the ones that you really want avoid).

Finally, it is in the area of rela-onships (both male and female) at I have some of my biggest egrets. There are relationships at are life giving, and there are lationships that are life taking. ooking back, I realize I had evoted far too much time to the tter. It is often easy to become nmeshed in situations (romantic r otherwise) that are not particu-rly healthy. These relationships id not make me feel closer to hrist or better about myself. istead, they tended to become lfish, sapping my energies and aving me feeling bitter and rained. This is not to say that od will never put you in a tuation in which you will be ked to give more than you ceive. From time to time there e people he calls us to minister who cannot give back the care ey take from us. But these

instances are relatively few, and far more common are those situ-ations we get ourselves involved in that hurt us more than they help us.

How can you tell which rela-tionships are good? Believe it or not, this is not all that difficult, and the older I get, the easier it becomes. Christ tells us we will know the tree by its fruits (Matt. 7:16). A good relationship will produce the fruits of the Spirit discussed in Galatians 5 — love, joy, peace, patience, kindness, goodness, faithfulness, gentleness, and self-control. A bad relation-ship will display the works of the flesh — fornication, impurity, enmity, strife, jealousy, anger, and selfishness. If I feel closer to Christ and better about myself when I am with someone, and if the fruits of the Spirit are coming out more and more in the things we do (and not just what we say), then the odds are quite high it is a good relationship. I wish I had been more careful in college to cultivate these kinds of relation-ships and avoid the other. This would have freed up an incredible amount of time and emotional energy for activities that would ultimately have been much more edifying and productive.

2

The incomparable, unconquerable you

Confidence. My Webster's New Collegiate Dictionary has a lot to say about that word confidence; some that is confusing, some that is clear.

The feeling of having confidence, of feeling unconquerable, depends on where we place our confidence. Or, better yet, in *whom* we place our confidence. For many of us, our sense of self-confidence is like a roller coaster. Some days (or moments) we're on a high. But most of the time, we find our confidence plunging. Or we feel like we spend most of the time on the climb, slowly gathering confidence before we take another dip.

What's the problem? Why aren't we confident?

We have a five-year-old friend in our neighborhood, Kyle Mackenney. He's a buddy of our five-year-old Jeremy. Kyle begins most sentences with these three words, "The problem is ..." Kyle, the analyst. Kyle has probably not yet analyzed the issue of confidence but if he were to do so, he'd probably say there's a problem. "The problem is" we place our confidence in things, items, persons, appearances, and beliefs that can collapse. Some of us base our sense of confidence in how many *friends* we have and what they are like. Or our confidence lies in *"looking good,"* or getting good grades (or not getting good grades, depending on our friends), or in being good in athletics or music. Or we may base our confidence on *success*. If we're successful, we're confident. But a failure shakes that confidence and a crisis in confidence crushes us.

Basing a sense of confidence in friends, looks, or success is illusive. We may think it will last forever, but circumstances can and do change. Friends move or reject us. Looks change through an accident or aging. We may get in a school that's more competitive than we ever imagined, and we aren't as successful. We can get cut from a team or injured.

My good friend and associate, Ray Moore, tells a great story about confidence. Ray was in his senior year in high school, a starting center on the basketball team. He wasn't particularly big or quick but he worked hard. And he had confidence. All summer long he practiced on the court in his driveway he could dunk fairly well (which 10 or 15 years ago was not all that common in high-school ball). With the confidence inspired of hard work and new skills, Ray was looking forward to the season. In one of their first games, Ray's team traveled to a rural area where the local high school was to dedicate a new gymnasium. It was the first school in the league with glass backboards, and the townspeople were excited about their new facility. The gym was packed as the teams took their pregame warm-ups. Ray was ready. He decided to unveil his new shot. He dunked one. The crowd roared. He dunked again when his turn came. The visiting team now had their eye on this player.

Then Confident Ray decided to cut loose, to use the Big Move he had developed over the summer.

Now, Alice, let's get this straight. If Mark calls, you're here; if Dale calls, you're out; if Bill calls, you'll see him tomorrow; if Dan calls . . ."

His plan was to dunk, grab the rim, and swing out toward his teammates, just as he did at the hoop on his garage. And he did. Only one thing went wrong. The backboard could not sustain his acrobatics. Explosion! The backboard shattered, throwing glass all the way to the half-court line. Ray came down with glass exploding all around him, holding on to the orange rim, the net around his wrist. The new backboard was ruined.

At first, his teammates, the other team, and the fans were stunned. Amazed. Quiet. Then a ripple of noise was followed by a wave of sound. Ray was booed off the court. In fact, the whole team was booed. They couldn't continue the game with only one rim and one glass board. Ray's team drove home in silence. The next day Ray's picture was all over the local papers. But instead of a hero, he was a goat. His confidence was shaken. The next week those same opponents traveled to Ray's school and won big. They got their sweet revenge. Ray's confidence was shaken for weeks.

What happened? A situation changed. The dunk, instead of a weapon, became a curse. Ray Moore was booed instead of cheered, and his confidence suffered as a result.

What do we do when confi-dence proves so illusive? We have developed ways to sustain our confidence, some good and some negative. We either control, hide, or create.

First, *we may try to control our circumstances.* We take few risks and do only those things that make us look good. We move into areas where failure is minimized and where we know we can perform well, like taking easy classes. We are afraid to move into areas where we feel vulnerable, and our growth is retarded. I do this sometimes. I stay away from skiing and migrate toward racquetball, which I play well.

Or we hide our weaknesses. If we're in a relationship, we'll break it off first because we're afraid the other person will discover who we really are. We can't stand feeling insecure or rejected so we beat the other person to the "break up." We're afraid that when others discover our "warts," it will be all over. Then our confidence will be so shattered we'll never recover.

Or we create an outward facade of confidence We become overly concerned with looking cool. Acting cool. We become preoccupied with hair, clothes, weight. This, we believe, will give us confidence.

In the end these strategies for building and sustaining confidence prove futile. Why? Because we can't control our circumstances forever. Controlling leads to suffering. In relationships, our invulnerability leads to loneliness and insecurity because people can't know us. Our confidence is replaced by an awareness that we have failed in facing our strengths and weaknesses. Our preoccupation with externals finally makes us appear shallow. It saps the energy that is needed to reach out, care for, and be interested in others. As a result our relationships suffer and our lack of confidence escalates.

God's desire is for us to be deeply confident people. He wants us to have the confidence that in him we can overcome hard times and adverse circumstances. Jesus spoke of confidence when he said, "I have told you these things, so that in me you may have peace. In this world you will have trouble. But take heart! I have overcome the world" (John 16:33).

Peace in the midst of turmoil. A spirit of overcoming when others are just trying to survive. That's what Jesus wants for us.

But how do we get it? Where does it come from?

It is absolutely critical to realize that *God's kind of confidence begins on the inside*. It doesn't depend on carefully controlled

circumstances or constant success. It can't be shaken by human failure. It is not derailed by human weakness. With God's confidence, we don't have to control, hide, or create.

How does God build that confidence within us?

First, God begins by loving us. Romans 8:39 describes the extent of that love. "Neither height nor depth, nor anything else in all

creation, will be able to separate us from the love of God that is in Christ Jesus our Lord." Consider what this is saying. The Creator of the Cosmos, the Lord of All loves you. He loves me. God loves high-school graduates. He's crazy about eighteen- and nineteen-year-old people. He's committed to them. Dedicated to them. He wants the best for them. All the time. And nothing can separate us from that love once we put our faith in Jesus Christ. Imagine that.

It doesn't matter how we look, or whether we get a 4.0 or a 2.7, or if our best friend rejects us. Whether we drop out of school, see our parents go through a divorce, put on ten pounds, or buy used clothing at a thrift store. Nothing. *Nothing* can separate us from God's love. So we're secure. We're loved. And that's the start of genuine confidence building.

Second, God forgives us. Colossians 2:13 states, "When you were dead in your sins and in the uncircumcision of your sinful nature, God made you alive with Christ. He forgave us all our sins...." Not only are we securely loved. But we're ultimately forgiven. All our sins are forgiven. Not some. But all. Past. Present. Future. There is not one sin you can do or imagine that God can't and doesn't forgive. Guilt doesn't have to contaminate us. We're forgiven. That's a confidence builder.

Third, God gives us power. Not only does God love us and accept us and forgive us but he also gives us the power through his Holy Spirit to achieve. Paul writing to the Ephesians talks about this power. "Now to him who is able to do immeasurably more than all we ask or imagine, according to his power that is at work within us ..." (Ephesians 3:20). God's power is at work within us. Imagine that. God himself works within us more than we can ask or imagine. His power works at home and at school. It works on the job and in relationships. It works on the ski slopes, in the gym, and in the library. If that's not a confidence builder, I don't know what is. And Christ's power never fails. There is no power shortage with God.

Fourth, God gives us gifts. In Romans 12, Ephesians 4, and 1 Corinthians 12, the Apostle Paul tells us that we are all gifted by the Holy Spirit and that all the gifts are important to the Body of Christ. So we are gifted and important. The body cannot get along without us. Adults in the body can't get along without us. Parents, professors, kids can't get along without us. We're indispensable. We're incomparable. That's a confidence builder.

Finally, God strengthens us through trials and temptations. And as we overcome, we grow in confidence. James 1:2 - 4 says, "Consider it pure joy, my brothers, whenever you face trials of many kinds, because you know that the testing of your faith develops perseverance. Perseverance must finish its work so that you may be mature and complete, not lacking anything." Mature. Complete. Not lacking anything. Those are "confidence" words. We can face the

move from home, the competitive nature of school. We can face the hunt for a job, the failure in Russian class, the search for a career. We can face a close friend turning his/her back on us. We can face financial difficulties, term papers, final tests. And we will survive. In fact, we'll more than survive. We will be conquerors through God who is at work within us!

And this understanding of God's confidence can lead to a new view of ourselves.

Who are you? You are a child of God, loved, forgiven, accepted, empowered, gifted, mature and complete, not lacking anything. Sounds good, doesn't it? It's true. Underline it.

The problem is we've become so used to playing negative tapes of who we are based on how we feel, look, or perform. The negative tapes have sometimes drowned out the presence of God.

He just says it makes him feel good.

What should we do to stop this cycle of thinking? I suggest you begin a *thirty-day experiment* (I will too) of saying the truth. Practice daily overcoming the negative noise by saying the truth. As you begin your day say something like this:

"Lord, I come to you today tempted to devalue myself. Forgive me. Instead, I choose to believe you. I realize:

I am acceptable to you.

You love me.

I am forgiven and free.

Your power is alive in me.

I am gifted.

I am free to fail without being overcome by negativity.

I am a loving person through your power.

I am able to withstand temptation and overcome trials.

I thank you."

Speak these words to yourself several other times throughout the day. Write these words down, carry them in your wallet. Reflect on their truth. Fill your mind with these words. This isn't a "psych job." It's not a hype. Those words are true. This is how God sees you. You are filling your mind with the truth instead of listening and believing falsehoods the culture proclaims.

I have a list of affirmations I carry with me. When I become negative about myself or devalue myself or the contribution I can make, I dig out my statements of truth and remind myself of my worth based on who God thinks I am. I suggest you do the same.

How does this relate to the lack of confidence we sometimes have in certain tasks, no matter how monumental or small? Like my lack of confidence in skiing? I believe God relates to and is involved in every area of our lives. He is with me even when I ski. So here's how I think God's sense of confidence is applied to my feeble attempts at skiing.

First, I don't have to look good. I can risk looking bad, stupid, or uncoordinated because whether I fall or not, whether I wear the latest ski styles or not, I am still

acceptable to God, forgiven, and gifted. How I ski has nothing to do with who I am or how God feels about me or how much confidence I have. Second, if I really do trust God, I am more relaxed and, consequently, can ski better.

Third, my skiing doesn't have a lot to do with the major issues of life, such as my relationship to Christ and his desire to use me and my gifts. As we used to say when I was in high school, I don't have to "sweat it."

Obviously, I have many dimensions to my life that are important, much more than recreational skiing. And God meets me there as well.

We all need confidence as we move forward. Christ knows that. He knows where we live, where we go to school. He knows what we need and works in our lives to meet those needs. He is our great supporter, teacher, and friend. With Jesus Christ as the source of our confidence, we can move forward with confidence. We are incomparable and unconquerable because of him.

3

Title or testimony

Tony Campolo tells the story of a black preacher who one Sunday morning gathered recent college graduates from his congregation and congratulated them on their new status in life as college grads.

Then, according to Tony, the preacher thundered home a message to them. "You've got a decision to make," he told them. "Do you want a title or do you want a testimony? Now Pharaoh, he had the title. But Moses, he had the testimony. Goliath, he had the title. But David, he had the testimony. Now Jezebel, she had the title. But Elijah, he had the testimony. Now Pilate, he had the title. But Jesus, he had the testimony." And the fiery black preacher marched through Scripture, emphasizing again and again this issue of title and testimony. "And, children (that's what he called them), as you stand here today, you have a decision to make. Do you want to go for the title or do you want to go for the testimony?" And with that he sat down.

That's the decision we have to make going into our adult life. What are we going to shoot for? What do we want out of life? Is it merely a title? Or is it a testimony of God's work in our life? Are we going for the external trappings of success or are we aiming to be God's people?

Are we going to seek first his kingdom and righteousness and let the glory chips fall where they may? Or are we going to go for the glitter — the title, the money, the fame, the possessions?

Now obviously, I'm hoping you'll say, "Yeah. I'm going for the testimony. Forget the title." But if you do, know that you'll be fighting an uphill battle. You'll be like a salmon fighting its way upstream to the spawning pools. The world system will do all it can to force you to conform to its mold. But as Paul says in writing to the Romans, "Therefore, I urge you, brothers, in view of God's mercy, to offer your bodies as living sacrifices, holy and pleasing to God — this is your spiritual act of worship. Do not conform any longer to the pattern of this world, but be transformed by the renewing of your mind. Then you will be able to test and approve what God's will is — his good, pleasing and perfect will" (Romans 12:1,2).

The preacher was urging his graduates to please God, just as Paul had urged the Romans. And I'm urging you to go for it! Go for the testimony.

Now a title is not wrong in itself. I have lots of titles. I'm a University Ministries director. I'm a staff member of a large church. I'm a husband. A father. A friend. A neighbor. A certified Television-Awareness training instructor. I'm an aging jock. I'm a "former" lot of things. Former editor. Former director of operations for a film company. Former lifeguard and swimming teacher.

And when most of us introduce people to one another, we find it convenient and helpful to use titles. For instance, "Bob, I want you to meet Margie. She's an account executive with SeaFirst. Margie, this is Bob. Bob's a vice president of a computer firm in Bellevue."

And there is nothing wrong in accumulating a title in the pursuit of a job well done. My friend Rod Handley is a C.P.A., a certified public accountant. He worked hard through four years of college obtaining a degree in accounting. Then he successfully completed his C.P.A. exam. He deserves to be called a C.P.A.

But titles can be distracting. They can distract us from the real essence of a person. Rod, the C.P.A., is also an assistant state director for the Fellowship of Christian Athletes (how's that for a title?). One of his friends is Steve Peuller, who is a National Football League quarterback (another title). Steve is a humble guy who doesn't need to be recognized by his title. But when Rod introduces Steve to individuals and groups, he notices a big difference in how they respond. When he introduces Steve as just his friend, he gets one response. When he introduces him as a pro quarterback, he gets quite another. People are more impressed by the quarterback label than they are by "friend."

It's a question of focus and priority. What is your focus? Is it contribution or recognition? Are you trying first and foremost to make a difference in the world or are you aiming for the title behind your name? That's a tough question. And it's a tough issue to live with even when you've arrived at the right conclusion.

I work with hundreds of college students each year. I encourage all of my students to invest a year or two in short-term missions after graduating from college. I believe an investment of this type will help students discover their gifts, their strengths and weaknesses, and will teach them a great deal about another culture, about Christ, and about what it means to serve him.

But many students I've talked with have a difficult time even thinking about such an idea. They are convinced they need to get on track in their careers so they won't get behind their peers. In the race for title and prestige, they need to get off to a great start. They can't get behind. Now if they choose to plunge into a career because of the contribution they can make to others or because they will be better prepared in the long run for contributing to God's kingdom, I applaud their decision. But if the primary motivation is to get off to a fast start in the pursuit of the title and its trappings, I'm disap-pointed.

Rod Handley, the C.P.A., rose to a position of manager in the Se-attle office of one of the Big Eight accounting firms in the country in a relatively short time. He was making big bucks, with the poten-tial for making a lot more. But then Rod found himself, more and more, wanting to work full time, not part time, sharing his faith with high-school and college athletes. This desire eventually translated into full-time ministry, which meant Rod had to give up his position in the firm. The firm didn't want Rod to leave. But leave them he did to become an assis-tant FCA director and an intern with me in University Ministries. His salary dropped astronomically. His peers were baffled. But Rod wanted to contribute in this way. He chose testimony over title. And I applaud him.

God is not impressed with titles. Many of his key people did not have titles. What was Abraham's title when he started? Director of a New Nation? What was Moses' title? Or Noah's? When Paul first started his ministry, what was his? Later we called him an apostle. And Jesus — He never had a title. Although some called him "teacher," he was never the High Priest of the Jewish Nation, or Senior Pastor, or Chief of the Twelve.

The important thing to focus on is contribution. And to realize you're playing for an audience of one. In 1 Samuel 16:7 the Lord says to Samuel, "The Lord does not look at the things man looks at. Man looks at the outward appearance, but the Lord looks at the heart." Some of the greatest contributions you can make in this world may never be recognizable or earn you a title, but God will be pleased.

Rod Handley, in addition to being a C.P.A. and assistant state director of the Fellowship of Christian Athletes, was also a second team All-American football player in the small college ranks (more titles). When he was playing football, he says he used to play better when he knew certain people he respected were in the stands. He loved the attention and glamour sporting achievements allowed him. But one day his perspective changed. A teammate of his, a strong Christian, told Rod that to get enthusiastic about a game, he never had to rely on the crowd, the media, or even teammates and coaches. Rather this teammate said he concentrated on playing to an audience of one — Jesus Christ. The great thing about Christ was that he didn't just show up for the championship game. He was there for every practice. Realizing that Jesus was part of every situation allowed Rod's teammate to give a hundred percent in every situation no matter what the atmosphere seemed to be. Rod learned from

his friend how much God cared. And when Rod began concentrating on the audience of one, his performance improved.

What does it mean to concentrate on an audience of one? It means you answer to only one. You don't answer to the world, you answer to God. It means you strive for excellence in all you do because you're doing it for him and because he is always watching you. It means you seek first his kingdom and his righteousness. You strive to make a contribution first and foremost. If such a decision requires that you forfeit a title or the fast track, you make the decision and let the chips fall where they may.

Title or testimony? Where are you headed?

Now let's talk about taking some risks.

WHAT I'D

Mary L. Walker is the assistant secretary of the U.S. Department of Energy for Environment, Safety and Health. She oversees over 260 nuclear and 160 nonnuclear facilities. She graduated from Glendale High School (California) and the University of California at Berkeley. She attended law school at Boston College and UCLA and obtained her J.D. in 1973.

My high-school and especially college years were "exploring" years for me. Unfortunately, they were also the years I moved farthest away from Jesus Christ, whom I had accepted as my Savior while a young child.

Never one to readily accept authority, I questioned rules. Raised in a church whose members observed a strict code of do's and don'ts, I began drifting away from Christian fellowship during my teenage years. Not surprisingly, in college I had almost no Christian friends. I was a strong, disciplined student, and did well academically, but I did not apply these strengths to a study of the Bible. Staying away from God's family and his word stunted my spiritual growth, and I made many mistakes that could have been avoided. It is not without purpose that Paul counseled his disciple Timothy to "pursue righteousness, faith, love and peace, with those who call on the Lord from a pure heart" (2 Timothy 2:22). The people we choose to associate with will, for better or worse, affect our lives. Friends who have an eternal perspective will challenge us to have one too.

Through some difficult times God led me to see that my commitment to him was less than complete. While my commitment to academic studies paid off, it was only as a young professional that I finally gave God *all* of my life. And he made me see that as his child, I am a part of the "family" of believers and that I need spiritual "food" (his Word) and the positive influence of committed believers to grow and to produce in me the qualities that will reflect Christ to the world. Until I read *The Master Plan of Evangelism* by Robert E. Coleman, I never realized how strategic it was that Christ chose to spend the vast majority of his three-year ministry building himself into just twelve people. The apostles, as we know, changed their world for Christ.

If I could live those college years again with the knowledge I have now, I would like to think I'd make some changes. I would define my priorities differently and more clearly. To know God and to more fully commit myself to him would be first. (We trust *who* and *what* we know.) I would spend more time reading the Bible and reflecting on how my own growing knowledge of myself stacked up against what Christ (our example) is like. I would have shared these thoughts with God in prayer and sought his truth and his will for my life. I would have asked him for things I know he wants for me, such as a

heart for people. For the last few years, I've kept a spiritual journal where I record thoughts, desires, struggles, insights, and "new" truths God has taught me. This has helped me to see God's working in my life over time. I wish I'd kept one in college. Those are frontier years that bring lots of changes. A journal can help you trace your development and remember the lessons God is teaching you.

Lastly, I would have asked God for — and would have sought out — Christian friends who would challenge and encourage me and share with me as we pursued together the things of God. It was not until all these things came together in my life — a total commitment to God, a study of his Word, prayer, and believing friends — that I began to grow strong as a believer and to actively share my faith with others. God has helped me see that the most important thing I can do to make my life "count" is to know him and help others know him. Having seen my own life turned around by the love and power of Jesus Christ, it is my greatest joy to help others see the difference he can make in their lives. And a simple old saying has never left me: "Only one life; it will soon be past. Only what's done for Christ will last."

4

Risktaking

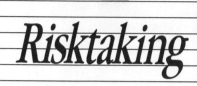

Do you remember the first time you ever rode a roller coaster at an amusement park? How you fearfully surveyed the ride from a safe distance, wondering if you could really ride it? Remember how you finally mustered up the courage and stood in line after buying the ticket? Excitement and energy mixed with doubts as the line drew closer to your car. And when the attendant buckled you in, you knew if you weren't secured, you'd be thrown to your death on the first plunge of the coaster. Do you remember asking the person next to you if anyone had ever died on this particular ride in this particular park?

And then the roller coaster took off, climbing, plunging, twisting, turning. When the ride was done, remember the laughter and the sense of accomplishment you had? And then how you got in line to do it again?

That was risk taking. Overcoming your fears to encounter a new experience. Pushing yourself to the edge. Taking that next adventurous step. Just think — if you had missed that opportunity because of your fears, you would never have experienced the thrill of the ride.

That's what risk taking is all about.

Risk, according to the dictionary, involves the possibility of loss or injury (that possibility existed to a slight degree on the roller coaster) or contains a dangerous element.

While the prospect of facing hurt, loss, or embarrassment is not fun, we have to take risks if life is to have meaning — and if we are to become all that God intends us to be.

Helen Keller, a wonderful woman who overcame major handicaps, once said that "life is either a daring adventure ... or nothing at all."

Jesus could have made the same remark. He implies this same truth when he told his disciples, "I have come that they may have life, and have it to the full" (John 10:10).

Abundant living involves immense risk taking. The Bible is filled with examples of people who took risks. Remember Noah in the early chapters of Genesis? He was asked to build a huge boat in a place where it had never rained. He was ridiculed by his neighbors. His immediate risk involved his pride, his reputation, his word with his family, and his confidence in how clearly he could hear God. But his primary risk was in missing what God had in store for him by not being obedient. In the end, the risk was worth taking.

A few chapters later, Abraham

also proved to be a guy who could take risks. God called him on a journey without a destination! Since Abraham was a rich man, he could have remained where he was. At least he knew what dangers he faced there. But when he heard God's call, he decided to take the risk. He embarked on an incredible journey and because of his faith, became the father of the Jewish people.

Remember King David before he was king? He was a mere shepherd boy who felt called by God to take on the giant Goliath. He risked being humiliated before his people and family. He risked being killed by Goliath. But had David not stepped forward with his sling and stones to face the incredible hulk, he would have risked missing what God had in store for him. So he took the lesser risk of facing the giant, and he won.

Sometimes we take risks and

don't win. At least not in our eyes. Several years ago, I felt as if God wanted me to embark on a small business venture that was designed to help youth workers around the country. I felt we had a good approach, a good "product," and that our motives were good. I knew it was a financial risk, but I wanted to follow what I considered to be God's call. I ended up losing a significant amount of money. So significant, in fact, that my family and I have been financially "catching up" ever since. It has made life uncomfortable at times and difficult at others. But I feel okay about it. I don't like the fact that I lost money and failed. But I like the fact I took the risk, that I tried to do what God wanted me to do, and that in the midst of the adventure, he taught me a lot. That's risk taking. No guarantees. If there were guarantees, it wouldn't be risky, would it?

Risk taking means stepping outside of our comfort zones, outside of what our peers may be doing, and committing ourselves to a new adventure.

But remember: There is a difference between intelligent risking and stupid risking. Let me give you an example. Years ago, my current boss, Bruce Larson, decided to learn how to ride a motorcycle. He felt he needed to break out of his mold, to do something different, something that even had a certain element of danger. But he also knew he had a family to love and support, a job to do, and a God to follow so he bought a medium-sized motorcycle and was on his way. That's intelligent risking. The risk stretched him, made him feel more alive but didn't kill him and deprive his family and friends of a beloved companion.

Several weeks ago we had a wonderful family in our church lose a son. He too took the risk of having a motorcycle. Only he had bought the most powerful, and he pushed it to the maximum. He lost his life in a crash. He was a strong Christian who had shared his faith with many. His grandma, who had no doubts her grandson was in heaven, wrote a poem about that accident and said that when he got to heaven, he would have to ask forgiveness for going too fast. He had driven fast, and he had left life faster than God probably intended for him. The risk was stupid. Intelligent risking means counting the cost, assessing the dangers and losses, and risking consciously and wisely. Stupid risking is pushing yourself beyond reasonable limits.

Here's another example. I love whitewater rafting. That, to me, is one of the most exhilarating experiences in life. But I don't white-water raft without a guide who knows the river — it's too danger-ous. And in case I fall overboard, I wear a lifejacket and a wet suit. And I know what to do if the boat should overturn and what to do if I should be trapped underneath the boat. There is risk involved, sure. But I've minimized some of the chances of fatality without depriving myself of the stretching, energizing experience that comes from being out on the whitewater. To do stupid risking would be to go down the river in my own one-man raft without a life jacket and a guide. The difference is clear, isn't it?

You may have already taken many risks in your life. You might have run for public office in school and subjected yourself to a popular vote. And you may have lost. I lost several elections in high school and college myself. You and I risked rejection. Maybe you turned out for a varsity sport or the school play, subjecting your-self to the whims of an audience. That's risky. You may have told someone you loved them; you made yourself vulnerable to an-other person. That too is risky. But think of the options. Think what you would have missed if you'd never taken any of the risks you have.

Christians, in particular, find a

new joy in taking risks and step-ping beyond comfortable bounda-ries. It is when we are led into situations we are not quite able to handle that we find the reality of

God and his presence in our lives.

Several years ago I stepped into a situation full of risks for me. After several years of not being on a church staff and working di-rectly with students, I became director of University Ministries at a church where they had previously had fantastic directors and where the ministry was strong. In a situation like that, it often seems your only option is failure. It's one thing to take over a situation where your predecessors had been flakes and where the program is in ruins. And another to begin a ministry from scratch. But I had stepped into a winning situation.

I remember the first night of fall quarter standing in front of hundreds of college students and thinking, "What a bright group of people. What if I fail? They'll eat me for breakfast." And I could have failed. But there was that thrill, that sense of exhilaration that God had called me to attempt this work for him. And, fortu-

nately, in this case, I risked and was not rejected. In fact, the job I'm now doing, this ministry with college students, has probably been the most fulfilling job and ministry I've ever had. If I had not taken the risk, I would never have been so blessed.

The great truth about risk taking as a Christian is that we don't take the risk alone. God is with us. Paul Tournier, the great Swiss psychologist says, "What gives life its unity is the knowledge of God. The true value of the adventure of action is not in what we do but in doing it with God, in entering into the creative adventure of God, in entering into intimate fellowship with him."

By taking risks we are entering into the adventure. With God. What a privilege. What fun.

Bruce Larson often says, "When God wants to teach you something, he takes you on a trip." Most trips involve risk. The risk of the uncomfortable.

One of my friends, Stu Harris, has traveled throughout Europe. He says, "I would rather spend a night in my own bed and wake to a warm shower and hearty breakfast than spend a sleepless night in a train station looking forward only to a long train ride and a single apple for breakfast. But there comes a strange sense of discovering new life when one is outside his comfort zone."

A life without risks, without stepping outside your comfort zone, is really no life at all. George MacDonald, the British author, says, "Low-sunk life imagines itself weary of life, but it is death, not life, it is weary of."

None of us want to live the "low-sunk life," I'm sure.

Tim Hansel is another friend who in his own words was "given a second chance of life." Tim, today, should be dead or a paraplegic at best. On a climbing expedition, he fell down a crevice and suffered a tremendous back injury. But he is alive and can walk. His accident has left him with a new-found joy in "truly living." He knows that each moment is here and then gone and that life is a gift. "Now is as good a time as any to jump in," Tim says. I agree.

We may all have tendencies to avoid risk taking but we are also drawn to it. We admire risk takers and appreciate their confidence. We know a new dimension of life is available to us when we set out to do a task that involves risk. The key is to listen and respond to our desire to take risk. When we repress those feelings and instincts we are paralyzed, and God wants us to be free.

So how do we begin taking risks? The beginning, I believe, is

to obey Christ. This first step may not involve risk taking at all. It may just be a nudge to clean your room or sit down and write an overdue letter or take that book and read twenty pages before bedtime. We must begin where we are, with the moment that is now. As we develop an attitude of obedience, we will be in a place where we can risk because we will be ready to respond when God calls us to more risky living. And, believe me, the life we live with Jesus Christ will be full of risks. If we begin now by saying yes to Jesus in the small things, we will continue to say yes in the risky things.

So here's to risk taking. Here's to life.

WHAT I'D

Dolphus Weary is president of Mendenhall Ministries in Mendenhall, Mississippi, a multifaceted organization that provides services in the areas of health, education, law, youth development, business, farming, recreation, and Christian education and nurture. Dolphus graduated from Harper High School in Mendenhall, Piney Woods Junior College, Los Angeles Baptist College, Los Angeles Baptist Theological Seminary, and the University of Southern Mississippi. He and his wife Rosie have three children.

If I could relive my college years, I would go straight from high school to a Christian liberal arts college instead of going first to a community college. I believe that would have given me a stronger foundation for the ministry I have today.

I probably would have chosen a less conservative Christian liberal arts college than the one I attended. My college was so conservative that everybody else was wrong, and nobody was right. It seemed as if no one fit their definition of a Christian. I would have gone to a school that was a little more liberal in terms of dress code and in the interaction between blacks and whites. The school I attended was so isolated that it isolated me from society in general and from the black community in particular. And there I was, a black student, preparing to go into a ministry that would deal with the needs of the poor and oppressed in our society!

I was greatly disappointed in my college because of the fact that a person like Dr. Martin Luther King, Jr., was made into an enemy of America. In 1968 when King was shot, I was sitting in my room listening to the radio, trying to figure out what had happened to my hero. In the hallway outside my door white Christian kids were talking about how glad they were Martin Luther King had been shot. I couldn't understand that then, and to this day, I still have difficulty understanding it.

If I had to do it all over again and if I had the choice, I probably would not have chosen to grow up poor. I probably would not have chosen to be born black and in Mississippi. But I have recognized over the years that my condition is not an obstacle that should prevent me from being the best I can be to the Glory of God. I have learned God can use me in spite of insurmountable circumstances I have had to face. I have learned that poor people who are born in ghettos and depressed communities all over the world can be overcomers because of the Lord. Our situation in life must not become an obstacle because God is capable of doing anything.

PART
TWO

NOW AND FOREVER
RESOURCES

The art of decision making

E very single day we are faced with numerous small decisions. What time should we get up? Should we get up at all? Should we eat breakfast before we shower or after? Should we shower? Should we eat? What shall we eat — Cheerios or Frosted Flakes? Should we brush our teeth? Which toothpaste shall we use? Shall we squeeze from the end or the middle? Which clothes to wear? What shall we eat for lunch, for dinner? Which television program should we watch? When should we study? What time should we go to bed? Some of these decisions were decisions our parents used to make for us. Now we make them. Big deal.

Often there are daily decisions that are more significant: whether to run with the crowd, to develop a friendship with a particular person, to join a Bible study, to rebel against your parents.

Then there are the monumental decisions that influence the direction of your life. What college should you attend? Should you take drugs? What about premarital sex? Should you marry him/her? What career to choose? Should you give your life to Christ?

From the small to the big, we are involved in decision making constantly. So the art of decision making is an important topic.

How do you make choices? And how can you know if the choices you made are the right ones?

Some people are overwhelmed by choices. Decisions are too hard to make. They vacillate in their decisions and then constantly second guess themselves once the decision has been made.

How can decision making be made easier? Here are some principles for making decisions my friends (including some recent high-school graduates) and I have put together.

Number One: **Who's Calling the Shots?**

The most important ingredient to successful decision making is your relationship to Jesus Christ. To be in a right relationship with him, you have acknowledged him as Savior and Lord of your life. You have decided to be his follower. But even though he is your leader and guide, you must still make decisions. The first and primary decision is: Who's calling the shots? If it's Jesus, then you are off to a good start in decision making. If your primary end is to be obedient to him and bring glory to God, then you're off to a good start in decision making.

Bob Munger, a wonderful pastor and writer, believes this is the big decision that affects all others. If we are united with Christ and seek to do his will,

most decisions (other than those God expressly requires or forbids — see Number Four below) will not make that much difference. He will use us and bless us whatever our decision. For instance, maybe you are struggling with the question of whether it is God's will that you go to UCLA or to Slippery Rock State. Bob's advice is to work through the decision carefully but to know that God will use you and bless you at either place. He suggests we should look at God's will as a train; it doesn't matter what car we're on (the engine, the caboose, or the dining car), what matters is that we're on the train.

The same principle holds with small decisions, of course. I don't think that God is concerned, for instance, about which toothpaste you use. Certainly he wants us to care for our bodies, since they are the temples of the Holy Spirit. Our responsibility, then, is to follow God's scriptural direction to keep up our health — and then to use our own best judgment as to which toothpaste to buy.

Number Two: **Begin with Trust.**

"Trust in the Lord with all your heart and lean not on your own understanding; in all your ways acknowledge him, and he will make your paths straights" (Proverbs 3:5 — 6). Maybe you've been quoted this verse before. When

you examine the words closely it seems your "own understanding" is meaningless, that what you think has no value. But that's not what that verse is telling us. What it means is "lean not on your own understanding *alone.*" In other words, trust in God and bring him into the decision-making process. Acknowledge the fact that you want to do his will, and you're interested in his insight. You are not going to act alone, independently from him; you're not going to rely on your own understanding *alone* and *apart* from Christ. Your own understanding and experiences are crucial to decision making as long as you don't rely on them alone.

Another emphasis of this particular Proverb is that we are to acknowledge God in everything we do. If we are not afraid to publicly acknowledge that Jesus Christ matters in our life and that our desire is to live a life that pleases him, he honors that. One way God honors our acknowledgment of him is by helping us make wise decisions. The person in right relationship with Jesus is a better decision maker than the person without Christ.

So trust that God is at work in the decision-making process as you wrestle with choices. You may not sense his help directly but trust the fact he's involved and wants what's best for you.

Number Three: **Pray.**

Praying is so obvious a suggestion. But have you prayed about the decision you need to make? Approach God humbly and ask him for help. Talk with him and think the decision through with him. And pause and listen.

Number Four: **Look at the Bible.**

The Bible includes some do's and don'ts that help in decision making. Let's look first at the do's. One example, Romans 12:14-16, says to "bless those who persecute you; bless and do not curse. Rejoice with those who rejoice; mourn with those who mourn. Live in harmony with one another. Do not be proud, but be willing to associate with people of low position. Do not be conceited." There are a lot of do's here. We are told to bless those who give us trouble, not take revenge. We are told to be involved with people, to share their joy and sorrow. We are told to do all we can to live in harmony with people. These principles should help us make decisions. They should make us ask ourselves: Are we blessing our enemies? Do we enter into the cares of others? Are we doing everything we can to live in harmony? Is this particular decision going to lead to greater or lesser harmony with others?

There are also some don'ts. God consistently tells us things we shouldn't be doing, not because he wants to deprive us of fun, but because he knows in the long run they are for our good. For instance, he says, "Don't get involved in illicit sex," that is, sex *before* or *outside* of marriage. If you're in a situation where you're tempted to engage in illicit sex, the decision has already been made by God. You don't even have to bother to ask. The answer is — *don't!* (The hard part here is carrying out the decision.)

There are many passages where what we are not to do is made clear. Colossians 3:9 is an example: "Do not lie to each other...." But there are gray areas which the Bible does not specifically address. For instance, the Bible doesn't talk about dancing,

social drinking, smoking, gambling, or working as a cocktail waitress. And what makes these areas even more confusing is that parents, churches, pastors, and other students have varying opinions. What do you do in the gray areas? Here are twelve suggestions for dealing with the "grays."

Number One: **Focus on the goal of 1 Corinthians 10:31.** "So whether you eat or drink or whatever you do, do it all for the glory of God." Ask yourself if your actions bring glory to God.

Number Two: **Remember as a Christian we have liberty.** We are free from the bondage of sin. We are no longer slaves to sin. But with limited time and resources we have to choose which path to take. The question is: Does the decision match the goals

I have for my life? Does this line up with what I really want to do?

Number Three: **Remember that love for others is a consideration in the decisions you make.** 1 Corinthians 8:9 says, "Be careful, however, that the exercise of your freedom does not become a stumbling block to the weak." In verse 19 of the next chapter, Paul writes, "Though I am free and belong to no man, I make myself a slave to everyone, to win as many as possible." In other words, Paul doesn't want to hamper anyone by what he does. Rod Handley, the CPA I mentioned in the last chapter, made a decision in high school that he believes prevented him from being a stumbling block to others. He decided he wasn't going to drink, not because the Bible strictly forbids it, but because he wanted to be an example to his friends. He says, "It was easier on my witness to make a stand in one direction than to waver back and forth with my words and actions. I didn't want to make people stumble in their search for Christ. I'd give up anything if it meant I could help someone find Christ."

A Christian friend of Rod's, Ken Hutcherson, is a guy who doesn't drink alcohol either. But he did greatly enjoy Coca-Cola, until one day he was challenged by a nonbeliever who told him he seemed to be addicted to the stuff. The nonbeliever felt Ken was being hypocritical. So Ken decided to give up the thing he enjoyed, Coca Cola, to set an example. And as it happened, Ken's denial was instrumental in the person who had challenged him eventually coming to know Jesus Christ.

Number Four: **Build up, don't break down.** Hebrews 10:24 says, "And let us consider how we may spur one another on toward love and good deeds." Ephesians 4:29 adds, "Do not let any unwholesome talk come out of your mouths, but only what is helpful for building others up according to their needs, that it may benefit those who listen." Building up. Benefiting. Let your decisions build up others, not tear them down.

In summary, use Scripture in decision making in the following ways. Decide if there is a clear do or don't guideline in Scripture. If there is, act accordingly. If it's a gray area, use the four principles just presented.

Number Five: **Try to Take a Step Back.**

If possible, remove yourself from the situation as best you can. Try looking at the situation from someone else's perspective. For instance, you're dating a guy who has a bad reputation. There has

been evidence that he may be cheating on you. You've heard about his past yet when he's around you he seems so nice and loving. You're obviously emotionally involved, and it's tough for you to make a decision whether to continue to see him. Try to step back and logically consider your thoughts. Get some fair and impartial friends (not those who hate him or love him or would like to be dating him) to look at the situation too. Look at the long-term effects of your decisions. Does it make sense?

Number Six: **Get counsel from people you respect.**

Talk to people who are wise, people who have had some experience, preferably wise,

mature Christians who have encountered similar situations.

Number Seven: **Try and envision what Jesus would do.**

Would Christ approve of your decision? Would you be embar-

rassed to have him see the results of your decision or be involved in the outcome of your decision? LeRoy Eims in his book, *Be The Leader You Were Meant To Be*, says that one way to be more Christlike and to know what Jesus would do is to get into the Bible. We can do that by hearing the Bible preached, by reading it, by studying it alone and with others, and by memorizing Scripture. By immersing ourselves in the Bible we are able to fill our hearts and minds with the actions and attitudes of Christ. Eims says, "The ones who do this will find them-

selves in touch with God, and he will guide them in decisions."

Number Eight: **Use the Pros and Cons, Plus and Minus Method.**

Whenever I have a decision to make, I get out a fresh sheet of paper, and at the top of the page, I write down the issue. For example, this year I was faced with the question, "Should I lead a group of students on a mission trip to Latin America during our Christmas vacation?" Then I draw a line vertically down the middle of the paper. On the left side, I write the pros (the advantages for going), and on the right, I write the cons (the disadvantages). Some of the advantages for making this trip were: the opportunity it presented for helping others come to know Christ; it meant a great time with students and an adventure in a different culture. The cons for the trip meant being away from family during the holidays; it meant no break from students; it required some extra work and preparation that would mean falling "behind"; and then there was the problem with the language barrier. Now, once these kinds of things are listed on paper, I am better able to assess the situation and make my decision.

By the way, in the end I finally decided to make the trip and with my family's wholehearted support. It was a great experience — but the *cons* were true. I was apart from family, I was fatigued, I was behind. Still, it was a great experience, our students were blessed, and many Latin Americans came to know Jesus.

Number Nine: **Go with your gut.**

If you can't make a decision and the answers aren't clear, go with your gut feelings. Pick the direction you think and feel you should go and give God plenty of opportunity to confirm or alter that course. (Note: This is sometimes scary.)

Number Ten: **Learn from your past experiences.**

Often you will encounter similar situations throughout your life. You may want to write down key thoughts in a tough decision-making process now that may help you in decisions you'll be faced with down the road.

Number Eleven: **Relax.**

The Lord loves you. He'll take your decision if it's made prayerfully, sincerely, and wisely, and use whatever you decide.

Number Twelve: **Keep moving**.

A rudder is useless if the boat is not moving. God wants to guide. But he can't guide an immobile person.

Those are a few principles in decision making. The bottom line: Love the Lord your God with all your heart, mind and strength and your neighbor as yourself and relax. God will help you make decisions, and he will bless you abundantly in what you decide.

Now let's take a look at an area of life where decision making is crucial. That area? Temptation.

WHAT I'D

Going to college a thousand miles from home was an important step of independence for me. But with independence comes responsibility, and I had some lessons to learn about money management.

When I arrived at school, I had $800 — hard earned that summer. It was my spending money for the entire year. To me, $800 was an enormous amount. I couldn't imagine it ever being used up.

I opened my first checking account, got the checks with the scenic pictures on them, and set out to enjoy my newfound fiscal freedom. I bought some clothes, and some things for my dorm room, and stocked up on the everyday essentials. I wasn't extravagant, but I wasn't restrained either.

About a month later, when it came time to balance my checkbook, I was stunned to discover I had spent almost half of the money in my account! Where had it gone? A pair of earrings, a new blouse, a record, a throw rug. They all added up. It was my first moment of reckoning with finances. I quickly put on the brakes, and needless to say, life was a lot more austere from then on.

Earning enough money each summer for my year's expenses

was always a hassle. After days of job hunting, the positions I landed offered little challenge and even less pay. I worked as a waitress, exercise instructor, and shoe salesperson. I even sold encyclopedias for one miserable week.

A high-school friend did it differently. Sally also headed off to college, but unlike most of us who dabbled in a variety of freshman courses, she spent the entire year in the Dental School. When summer rolled around, she was a certified dental assistant and was quickly hired by a local dentist. Every summer her job was waiting for her, and she made three times more money than most of us.

Of course, there was a cost to Sally's decision. She was in school a year longer to get her degree, which, incidentally, was not related to dentistry. But the lesson was clear: a marketable skill is the ticket to landing a good job. Sally never worried about getting that paycheck.

Not so with me. One summer, I was working in a chicken and ribs restaurant, and had figured out that I would not make enough money to cover my regular expenses for the upcoming school year. That night I tossed and turned and could not sleep. (I have since learned that God often

gives me a restless night when he wants to get my attention.) At about 3 a.m. I got up and started reading my Bible. As I read, I felt God was telling me to give a portion of my earnings away. Can you believe it? Here I was, making less than ever, and God wanted me to voluntarily give it up. Even so, I went to sleep with a new peace.

I have never regretted tithing, or giving back to the Lord a portion of my earnings. Instead it has been an important reminder that God provides for all my needs. It is a test of his goodness every paycheck, and he is always faithful. The summer I began tithing, I actually earned more money than I thought possible, enough to last through the year.

I know it was God's grace that I learned these lessons when I had very little. Thankfully, my income now exceeds $800 a year, but I know the first step in being faithful with a lot, is being faithful with a little.

Susan Hutchison is the anchor/managing editor of KIRO Eyewitness News, a CBS affiliate in Seattle, Washington. She graduated from Annandale High School in Virginia and the University of Florida.

6

Temptation

scar Wilde once said, "I can resist everything but temptation." All of us have probably felt this way too. It seems we can resist some temptations, since we're not weak in every area, but in other areas we are particularly vulnerable. We can resist only for so long before our resolve collapses, and we succumb.

Martin Luther, the great reformer, once made a statement I often quote when talking about temptation. "You can't stop the birds from flying around your head but you can stop them from making a nest in your hair." We can't stop temptations from coming our way but we don't have to give in to them. That's the message of the Bible. We can live life without losing in the temptation battle.

I've done "temptation surveys" with high-school and college students, asking them, "What are your greatest temptations?" The list is familiar.

In my most recent survey I asked 173 collegians (men and women, upper and lowerclassmen) what their three greatest temptations were. Here's the response I received.

The number one temptation for them was lust. Sixty-six of those surveyed listed it as one of their top three temptations. If you combine those who said "lust" with those who were tempted to have illicit sex, the number was 104! Out of 173 students, 104 listed lust and sex as one of their top three! Number two on the list concerned the subject of eating, either the temptation to overeat or to undereat. Gluttony, obesity, anorexia, and bulimia are all problems that arise in this area of temptation. Number three was the temptation to procrastinate (I may have given this survey too close to finals!)

Other temptations listed in past surveys include the temptation to cheat, to lie, to take drugs, to get drunk, to commit suicide, to get revenge, to run from God, to take the easy way out, to gossip, and to slander. You name an area of conflict, it probably appeared in the survey.

But what does the Bible say about temptation? James 1:13 -15 gives a vivid presentation of temptation. "When tempted, no one should say, 'God is tempting me.' For God cannot be tempted by evil, nor does he tempt anyone; but each one is tempted when, by his own evil desire, he is dragged away and enticed. Then, after desire has conceived, it gives birth to sin; and sin, when it is full-grown, gives birth to death." James is saying, first, that God doesn't tempt us. So we can't blame him. I've heard people say, "Well, I guess God just made me too weak to handle this. He understands, he created me. He knows I have to give in eventually to this temptation." That's crazy! God doesn't tempt us, and although he under-

stands our struggle he doesn't expect us to give in and fail when temptations — whatever they may be — arise.

And we can't blame our inability to handle temptation on our parents or on the way we were raised. That isn't what James is saying either. What he does say is that temptation is a deadly process. He likens it to childbirth. But in the case of temptation, the birth process doesn't bring life, it brings death. That's quite a contrast.

William Barclay, the late, great British teacher and scholar, said, "There is a civil war raging inside every person." James tells us this is caused by our own evil desire: a wrong desire is conceived, acted upon, and the result of this union of desire and action is sin.

Notice that *temptation itself is not sin. Giving in to temptation is.* The Bible says that Jesus was tempted in all ways. In 1 Corinthians, Paul talks about temptation. Everyone is tempted. It is acting on this temptation that is sin. I stress this fact because I've seen young Christians who are convinced they are outright sinners because they've been tempted. That's not the issue. Giving in to temptation is.

In 1 Peter 5:8 more light is shed on the subject of temptation: "Be self-controlled and alert. Your enemy the devil prowls around like a roaring lion looking for someone to devour." Satan knows our weaknesses, so we need to be alert and self-controlled. It all comes back to evil desires. We have them, Satan exploits them, and we are tempted. So what do we do when we are tempted? Here are some steps that have been helpful to me and to others.

1. Take personal responsibility. From the beginning, admit that you are ultimately responsible for the choices you make. God isn't tempting you. It's your responsibility!

2. Remember God has gifted us and equipped us for the battle with temptation. 1 Corinthians 10:12-13 talks about how we've been equipped, and in verse 12 Paul reminds us to be ready. "So, if you think you are standing firm, be careful that you don't fall! No temptation has seized you except what is common to man. And God is faithful; he will not let you be tempted beyond what you can bear. But when you are tempted, he will also provide a way out so that you can stand up under it." Some great principles are contained in this verse. Here are some:

• One of God's gifts is readiness. He encourages us to be self-controlled and alert. He warns us that a fall is only moments away.

• Not one temptation that we encounter is so unusual that no one has faced it before. With that encouragement, we can face our own temptation knowing that others have. Misery does love company even in temptation.

• God is faithful; he has promised to be with you. You are not alone.

• God will provide a way out. You won't be tempted beyond what you can bear. Christ's power is always there for us, and the temptation will never overwhelm the power of Jesus. Sometimes the way might involve common sense — like running from a situation. At other times, it might appear as superhuman resolve. At other times, it may even be a divine interruption (the phone might ring or your parents might appear) or divine intervention (it seems almost like a miracle but somehow God gets you out of the situation.)

Now what are some specific suggestions for dealing with temptation? There is one step we need to take which I call *purposeful resignation*. It's when you reach the point you admit you need help,

when you decide to rely on the resources of the Lord. It's basically a way of admitting the truth of John 15:5, that "apart from me (God) you can do nothing," and of Philippians 4:13 when Paul says, "I can do everything through him who gives me strength."

The second suggestion deals with specific kinds of temptation like lust, the desire to take revenge, some eating disorders, and anything else that involves images. I call it *image displacement*. The Bible says, "If the eye is sound, the whole body is sound." So what we see, we are apt to react to. If you are careful with what you view, your actions will be sound and correct. But if you're not, you'll likely have problems. Let's get specific. Lust is fueled by images. You see a good-looking body in person or in books, movies, or magazines, and your mind has some specific images to lust after. So what do we do to keep the fuel of lust from burning out of control? I suggest we edit the magazines we read, the films we see, the books we read.

At one time in my life, I did movie reviews and, in the course of a year, saw many films. I realized they were having a subtle effect on my values. When God got hold of me in these areas, he began to prune back the number of films I saw.

I also think it's important to edit our conversations. If our conversations are filled with sexual innuendo, if we're always talking about how much we "got" from someone (believe me, some girls play this game too), our conversation needs to be seriously edited.

Desires can be nourished or stifled. If you keep an image or desire in your mind long enough, it will eventually lead to some sort of action. And if we happen to fail, Satan likes to run "instant replays" of our failure and sin to shake our confidence in standing firm. Or if we succeed in stifling an evil desire and overcome a temptation, he is sure to remind us of the fun we might be missing as a Christian. So when ungodly images appear in your mind, displace them with positive ones. When you have a lustful thought, imagine Christ walking into the situation. See Jesus entering the image. Or conjure in your mind the image of Jesus on the cross and remind yourself he died to keep you from being enmeshed in sin. Or displace one thought with another one, spiritual or not. For instance, if a lustful thought comes into your mind, think of something pleasant from childhood.

Another practical method of dealing with sins of action — illicit sex, lack of discipline in any area, a desire to run from God, or procrastination — is *personal or group accountability*. Tell others what you're struggling with and ask them to hold you accountable. Being in a small support group is helpful because the people in your group can check up on you and help you. When I was in a losing weight mode a year or so ago, I had a friend who was also trying to shed a few pounds. We agreed to work together; we agreed we would encourage each other and check up on one another to see how we were doing. That was helpful. One time some rich home-made chocolate chip cookies were

being served with chocolate chip mint ice cream for dessert. I called my buddy to get some support, "Help, Bruce, they're serving dessert!" And he helped me refrain, as I did him when he faced the same temptations.

In real estate there is an old adage: the three most important characteristics of a property are location, location, location. *Location* is also crucial when it comes to temptation.

I know of a fine Christian couple who were engaged to be married. Their engagement period still had several months to run before the wedding, and they knew they were in danger of being overcome by passion to the point of sexual intercourse. They realized almost every date was ending up on the sofa in his apartment, and they were close to making love. They went to a friend, seeking his advice. He told them that from that point on until the time they were married, they should confine their dating to a Denny's Restaurant. (Isn't it amazing how few people make love in a coffee shop?) They had no choice but to sit across from one another and just talk. It turned out to be a great solution. This couple still loved each other. They still had the hots for each other. They still were spending time together. But they weren't in danger of giving in to the temptation of premarital sex because they had changed locations! So they were safe. The lights, the other people, the waitresses, the booths, and tables prevented them from giving in. They concluded their engagement period as virgins. Location helped them run the race well.

Location works for food temptations too. If you have a tendency to overeat, it's important that where you study, relax, or sleep does not have a stash of food. Or if procrastination is a problem, you'll want to study in a place almost distraction-free so there's nothing else you can do but study. Location is important.

Here's another suggestion for dealing with temptation — the three words, *run, run, run*. Running from temptation is not a sign of weakness. It may be a sign of great wisdom. Do you remember the story of Joseph? How he was sold into slavery by his brothers and eventually became the head of the household of a man named Potiphar, an officer in Pharaoh's army? Potiphar's wife, as you know, became keenly interested in Joseph and encouraged him to make love with her. He steadfastly refused. Finally, one day she trapped Joseph in her room, but he did the only thing he could — he ran. Potiphar's wife managed to rip Joseph's coat off him and later used the coat as evidence against him by accusing him of rape. But Joseph had done the right thing. And God honored his ability to run, run, run.

Another Old Testament hero, David, did the opposite. He stayed when he should have run, and he suffered immeasurably for it. In his story, he was at home when he should have been at war. It was a warm spring night, and he was on his palace roof, surveying his kingdom when he noticed a beautiful woman taking a bath. Now there was probably nothing he could do about seeing the woman once. But David called his advisor and asked who the woman was (he was adding information to his image), and then he invited her to his home (another bad move in fighting temptation). She arrived, and they made love. When she became pregnant, the temptation led to more sin: David had her husband murdered to cover up what he had done. But in God's scheme of things, no one can ever completely cover up his sin. David should have run, but he chose to fuel his evil desire. "Then, after desire has conceived, it gives birth to sin; and sin, when it is full-grown, gives birth to death."

The key to the problem of temptation is that we don't have to give in. We can keep birds from making a nest in our hair. We can rely on the resources of God and his practical suggestions for dealing with temptation, and we can win. Regardless of how well you've done in fighting temptation in the past, claim God's purpose for you in the *present* and in the future. Remember God will never allow you to be tempted more than you can bear, and with each temptation, he'll provide a way of escape. That's the good news.

But what happens if there's bad news? What happens when we fail in the temptation battle or when others fail and hurt us deeply? That's the subject of the next chapter's discussion on forgiveness.

Bruce Bailey

Bruce Bailey is a self-employed designer. He designs any and all. He's also deeply involved in ministry with college students. He graduated from Lincoln High School in Seattle, Washington. After a few weeks at the University of Washington, he quit to develop a career in business and communications. He and his wife, Gay, have two married daughters.

B y the time I became a successful business and communications consultant in my mid thirties, I was known as "The Dozer" — a nickname I was proud of. I got a lot done and I didn't take no for an answer. I was heading for the fast lane to fame and fortune.

"Hey! If God can move mountains, so can I!" That was my life for years. When the uselessness of trying to build what time will destroy finally caused me to turn the driver's seat back over to him, I discovered that his work was a labor of love instead of a drive for power. And that, more often than not, it went slowly in his garden, slowly and gently, one weed, one seed at a time.

I am not trying to be flip when I say that from atop my "ladder of hindsight " I wouldn't change a thing — *but* I would let God change anything and everything he wanted.

I had lived a life of control. A lust for power was my problem, a problem that denies authority and eventually results in "crash and burn." It is a problem that you face, too, as young achievers, young men and women seeking the right choices for your life. Achievers love measurable accomplishment, successful ventures; to change things, to control their environments, make things happen, get things done.

Being a controller is not being self-controlled. That's the stuff of the Holy Spirit in maturing Christians who desire obedience instead of "getting away with it," who desire purity before pleasure, and eternal gifts instead of instant gratification. Self-control produces growth. If we are living in the light, if we're getting pruned as needed, if we are willing to receive the water and fertilizer we must have to grow tall and strong, then, in season, we will produce fruit. This is the disciplined and obedient life of the Christian exercising self-restraint or control, the right kind. A life directed by God.

My problem was one of motivation and attitudes. I didn't really believe God had the best plan for my life. I was not prepared to try all the wonderful things life has to offer, looking to him for guidance and reaching out to others with his joy. I was afraid to let go of the comforts of ambition and upward mobility. (Isn't it clever of the Devil to call that slow easy descent into destruction "*upward* mobility"? Now my motives and attitudes are different.

What about a few things I would do the same (with a change of motivation)? Sure, there are a few I can recommend. Learn a tough sport, sail an ocean, get married, have babies, grow old with your mate, make a movie, take an opera class, lose some weight, eat dessert first, try hard at something and fail miserably at it, write a song and sing it in a crowded elevator, start a business, design your dream house and build it, fast for ten days, change professions, tell a stranger about Jesus, laugh until you cry, cry until you laugh, hire somebody, fire somebody, obey your favorite memory verse for a month before you memorize another (how about one day?), wink at an old person, ask forgiveness for something secret you did a long time ago, tell God "Send me."

Mainly, stick with Jesus. Live fully. Christ invented freedom so that he could set you free. Your enemy wants you bound up in chains of "I can't," and "I wish I hadda," and "I shoulda-coulda-woulda." He wants you spouting that garbage for the rest of your lives. But if you stay close to Jesus' heels you will have few regrets.

7

Forgiveness as a way of life

In chapter six, we discussed the subject of temptation. The bottom line was that we will be tempted. Temptation in itself is not a sin. We don't have to give in to temptation. Through the great resources of God, we can win in the battle with temptation and sin.

But what happens if we blow it? What happens if we give in to temptation and sin? Is it all over for us? Is our relationship with Jesus Christ ruined? Are we considered outcasts in Jesus' sight? Do we become second-class citizens in the kingdom? The answer to each of those questions is an emphatic no. God is a very realistic God. "Grace and truth" describe him well. The "truth" is that we can win over temptation; God doesn't want us to fail, and we don't have to fail. "Grace" is that if we do fail, he has a provision for our sin — that provision is *forgiveness.*

But forgiveness is not only our provision when we fail. It's our provision when others fail and hurt us deeply. It works two ways. When we sin, we *receive* forgiveness. When we are sinned against, we *extend* forgiveness. In both cases, forgiveness frees us. Lack of forgiveness weighs us down.

My wife likes to tell the story of the little boy who went to the church picnic. His parents couldn't go so he made his own "picnic lunch" — one stale, bologna sandwich. When he got to the picnic, he saw a feast. An unbelievable spread. Sliced ham, roast turkey, molded Jellos, fresh doughnuts, apple pie, homemade ice cream, juicy hamburgers, chocolate cake, soft drinks, punch, chocolate chip cookies. But he clung to his bologna sandwich. He wanted to help himself to what was on the table but he couldn't. He didn't feel like the feast belonged to him and, besides, he had his lunch, one he had made himself — his very own stale, bologna sandwich. It was *his* regardless of how stale it was. But one of the ladies at the picnic saw the young boy clutching tightly to his paper sack and invited him to join her family for lunch. He said, "No thank you. I have my own." And then she made a great and wise gesture. "I'll tell you what. Let's make a trade. You give me what's in your sack, and I'll give you what's on this table." And with that, the trade was made, and the boy enjoyed the feast.

The story of the stale bologna sandwich is a parable of forgiveness. The sandwich represents our guilt and bitterness — the stale aspects of life — that we carry around with us if we haven't experienced the giving and receiving of forgiveness. The feast —

the cake, the burgers, the ham, the pie — represent the riches God has for us when we experience his forgiveness in our lives and extend it to others.

None of us wants to go through life clutching a brown paper bag with a stale bologna sandwich

when we can enjoy God's feast. But unless we understand the dynamics of forgiveness, we don't have access to the feast.

Forgiveness begins at the cross where Jesus Christ was crucified. Colossians 2:13-15 says, "When you were dead in your sins and in the uncircumcision of your sinful nature, God made you alive with Christ. He forgave us all our sins, having canceled the written code, with its regulations, that was against us and that stood opposed to us; he took it away, nailing it to the cross. And having disarmed the powers and authorities, he made a public spectacle of them, triumphing over them by the cross."

What the apostle Paul is saying to the church at Colosse and to all of us is that if Jesus had not died on the cross, we would be hopelessly dead in our sins. Sin would overwhelm us. We would be overcome by our sin, our bitterness, our guilt. But Jesus has freed us from that by dying on the cross. When we respond to him, inviting him to enter our life to become our Savior and Lord, we are totally pardoned. Forgiven. Our sins are erased. The psalmist says in Psalm 103:12, "as far as the east is from the west, so far has he removed our transgressions from us." Because of the cross, God sees us in a new light. We are forgiven people in right standing with him.

Jesus' death on the cross also means he has freed us up to be forgiving people. We need, on an *ongoing* and *daily* basis, to extend and receive the forgiveness that God has given us. God wants us to live clean, unhindered lives. When we are not forgiving toward others we are burdened; we can't communicate with God as well. Lack of forgiveness leads to disharmony between ourselves and God, and between ourselves and others.

Let me give you an example. When my wife and I have hurt

each other by our words or by our actions, communication breaks down. The hurt and anger burden us, and we can't enjoy the great relationship God intended for us when we got married. We have discovered how very important it is that we ask for, receive, and extend forgiveness with each other. When I say, "Forgive me for what I've done," and Marilyn says, "You're forgiven," the action of forgiveness cleanses me and frees us to get the relationship back on track. Now we may not immediately feel good about each other but we have laid the foundation for a healthy relationship. We know that our communication will not be excellent unless we ask forgiveness of one another.

Forgiveness is also of great importance in our relationship with God. When we don't confess our sins, communication is hindered. Our relationship with him suffers. 1 John 1:9 has been referred to as the "Christian's bar of soap" because of its cleansing power: "If we confess our sins, he is faithful and just and will forgive us our sins and purify us from all unrighteousness."

Confession leads us to experience forgiveness. Forgiveness is God's disposal system. Forgiveness rids us of the stress of the hurts we carry, the low self-esteem we have because we feel out of sync with the Father and with others. By confessing our sins and receiving God's forgiveness, we are free to grow and become all that we can be in Jesus Christ. Whenever we sin, it's important to confess immediately to God and receive his forgiveness. Some people call the method of immediately confessing sin and receiving forgiveness, "Spiritual Breathing." We *exhale confession,* we *inhale forgiveness.* We keep our "accounts short" with God and with others; we don't let the sun go down on the wrath of our unforgiveness and because of that, we move through life unburdened by sin and its consequences.

But many of us don't understand how forgiveness works. For some of us, we have not seen forgiveness modeled very well. Maybe we grew up in a home where our parents had a difficult time dealing with the need for forgiveness, for extending or receiving it. Maybe we grew up surrounded by people who avoided forgiveness or harbored grudges or ignored wrongs. Forgiveness may be a fuzzy subject for some of us. We need clarification. Better understanding. We need to get a handle on the dynamics of forgiveness so that we can be more forgiving people.

I think this chapter is especially crucial at this stage in your lives. You are moving into a life that can either be a great adventure or a devastating experience. You need to be a person who is free to see what God wants for you and to do it. That's the adventure. But if you're overwhelmed by the consequences of not understanding and practicing forgiveness, you'll be severely handicapped, and life will cease to be for you the adventure God intended it to be.

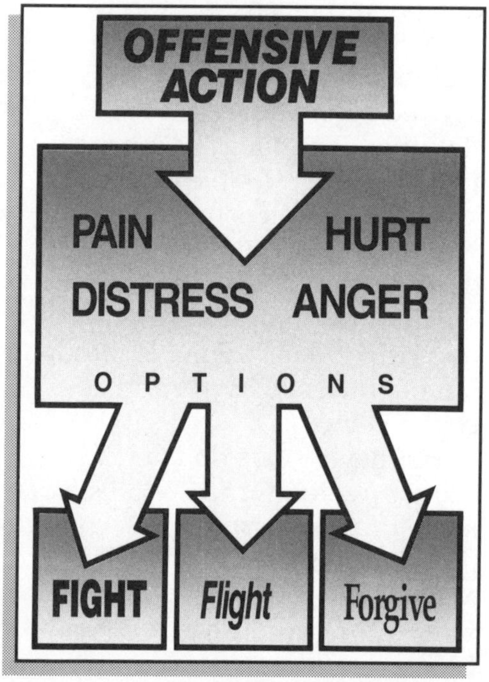

Practicing forgiveness concerns two vital areas of life.

1. The first is *what happens when we are hurt or offended by someone.* What happens when someone sins against us. Growing up, you have been hurt. In high school, people have, at times, sinned against you intentionally and unintentionally. What happens when you're hurt, and how do you deal with this pain?

Look at the diagram to the left. When we are hurt, numerous emotions come into play. We might experience *anger.* Or *pain.* Or both. The hurt triggers the production of adrenalin in our body. Our face might feel flushed. We know we have been injured.

You have three options in dealing with this pain. You can choose to fight and fume and lash out. You can work at getting even. That's one way to handle it. Or you can run away from the situation. And there are many ways to do that. You can soothe your anger with food, alcohol, or drugs. Or you can rebel and involve yourself in unhealthy

OFFENSIVE ACTION

PAIN   HURT
DISTRESS   ANGER

O P T I O N S

FIGHT | Flight | Forgive

relationships. There are many ways to flee. *Or* you can forgive.

Fight. Flight. Or forgive. These are the options. When you practice the first two, the painful experience most likely remains with you. The video screen of your mind replays the hurt, and your body reacts in the same way it did when you were first hurt. The body doesn't distinguish between the real and the replay. The lack of a forgiving spirit is hard on us physically and emotionally; the body heals and rebuilds itself in down times, but when you're regularly reliving old offenses there is no down time. Adrenalin continues to pulsate through your body. Healing is delayed.

What we need to do is forgive quickly. Forgiveness frees us from bitterness. The Bible says bitterness is like a cancer. The writer of Hebrews says, "See to it that no one misses the grace of God and that no bitter root grows up to cause trouble and defile many"(Hebrews 12:15). Bitterness not only causes us to miss the grace of God but it contaminates others. For our own well being and for the well being of others, we need to forgive and have God take away the bitterness that can consume us.

Forgiveness allows us to see the hurt in a new perspective. We

believe that God works for good in every situation (Romans 8:28), and we know he can take what was intended for evil and turn it into good (see the story of Joseph, particularly Genesis 45).

Forgiveness heals and restores us so we can get on with our lives. But what happens when for some reason we can't seem to forgive or we don't want to receive it? What happens when we can't confess our sins or ask for forgiveness or we feel too unworthy to receive forgiveness? John Bachelor of Burden Bearers, a counseling agency in Seattle, says, "We have an inner mechanism that tends to enforce an edict, 'Confess or Be Punished.' Either we must find a way to be punished or we will punish ourselves."

What are some of the ways we punish ourselves? What are some of the ways we deal with our sense of guilt?

We become *depressed*. Almost unconsciously, we *give in to guilt*, and we feel down.

Or we might *rebel*.

Or we might *rationalize*. "So what. It was not a big deal. Everyone does it. I'm no worse than any of the rest of them."

Or we *transfer the guilt to others*. We become *hypercritical* of what others are doing. One of the most critical times of my life was when I was harboring guilt for things I had done and tried to keep hidden. I became less critical when I finally dealt with my sin and made peace with God and attempted to make peace with others.

Or we try to make up for what we've done wrong by becoming *people pleasers*.

Or we *play a role*. We become the cool, detached one. Or the social critic. Or the humble servant.

Or we *deny we did anything wrong* to the point we almost believe our lie. But one of the Holy Spirit's jobs in our lives is to point out sin. Not to condemn us (remember, we've been forgiven through Christ's sacrificial death on the cross) but to free us and conform us to Christ's image.

Whatever the techniques we use to avoid receiving forgiveness, they are not satisfactory in the long run. But when we finally do

recognize our need of forgiveness and cleansing, how do we experience it? Here are some steps that have been helpful to me and to others.

1. **I go to God when I sin.** I recognize that asking for forgiveness and receiving it is a gift from God. I have access to forgiveness and the ability to forgive because of Jesus Christ. So I try not to snack on sins. I want to rid sin and the effect of sin in my life. I believe 1 John 1:9 and trust God to forgive me when I fail.

2. **I go to others when I offend them.** I ask for their forgiveness. I make restitution where I can. And if they won't forgive me? I still make confession to God; I do my part even though I can't control their response. God forgives me, I'm clean, and in humility and personal regret, I can

move on.

But what do I do when people I've hurt are dead, or I've lost contact with them, or they are too far removed from me (either physically or emotionally) for me to contact and ask forgiveness? Chuck Swindoll suggests in his book, *Improving Your Serve,* you find a Christian friend and confess to him, and let him extend Christ's forgiveness to you on their behalf. But even as you read this, don't put all the people you've ever hurt or will hurt into this category!

3. **I forgive others for their wrongs against me.** Forgiveness becomes a way of life for me. I become an aggressive forgiver. I remember in Matthew 18:21-22 when Peter asked Jesus how many times he must forgive, Jesus essentially told him, "You are to forgive an unlimited number of times."

I am able to be a forgiving person because I remind myself that:

a. I am a forgiven person in Christ (Romans 8:1).

b. The Great Forgiver, Jesus Christ, is alive in me.

c. I can proclaim, "I choose to forgive (   )." (List the name of your teacher, parent, friend, or "enemy.")

d. I yield the right to remember and recall this hurt. Once my wife, Marilyn, needed to forgive some

people. She struggled with this until one day her good friend Margie suggested they go for a walk on the beach. Margie dug a hole in the sand and gathered pebbles to be used as symbols for each of Marilyn's hurts. Margie told Marilyn to drop each rock in the hole and cover them with sand. Then Margie said, "Anytime you want to remember and recall these hurts, you will have to come back to the beach and dig them up." Enough said.

e. I trust God to work all things together for good (Romans 8:28).

f. I will bless the person I've forgiven as evidence of my for-giveness. To bless is to want the best for a person. To pray for and not persecute that person.

Let's practice forgiveness as a way of life and forget stale bolo-gna sandwiches forever.

8

How to have a quiet time

How would you like to have personal access to the most powerful and most wealthy and most wise person on earth? Anytime? How would you like that person to know you by name and spend as much time with you as you wanted? Anytime! How would you like this person to share his power and wealth and wisdom with you? And all you had to do was stay in touch. If this interests you, you'll love this chapter.

You've probably run into a few people in your life who suggested that you have a "quiet time." A time each day with the Lord. In my life the people who encouraged me in high school to have quiet time were my parents and a few pastors. I never had a friend suggest a quiet time was necessary for my life. But in my senior year in high school I got into the habit of a quiet time, and except for a few brief periods of spiritual inactivity, and except for missing a day here and there, I've had quiet times ever since. I think they've been very helpful to me, and I highly recommend them.

In fact, quiet times have put me in touch with the most powerful, most wealthy, most wise person not only on earth but in the entire creation! I've found they make a huge difference in my life. I've found them motivating, encouraging, strengthening, humbling,

refreshing. But I've not found them magical. I've heard people say, "If I don't have a quiet time, I have a bad day." That may be true. But I've had some bad days on days I've had a quiet time, and I've had some good days on the days I haven't.

Well, if they aren't magic or guarantees of a successful day, why have them? I asked this question of the college students in a small group with me. Here's what they said.

1. **"It's a great way to start the day."** I agree. I like to start the day with a quiet time. But I have a suggestion to make. Have a quiet time when it's best for you. Some people are not worth much in the morning. It may be best for them to end the day with a time with God. The main thing is to have a regular time to meet God.

2. **"A quiet time is an antidote to the hectic style of our lives."** All five guys in my small group are amazingly busy. Life has intensified, not slowed down, for them since high school. The demands of work, school, and relationships are great, and they have found that deliberately slowing down and listening to God is an amazing way to get a fresh perspective on things. It's good for the soul and good for the body. It's a chance to catch one's breath.

3. **"It's an opportunity to release some burdens you've been carrying."** When you sit

with God, you can pour out your heart to him. You can tell him about what seems too heavy to carry. You can confess your sins and feel the burden of guilt lifting. You can ask for advice. It is a unique opportunity to allow the Lord of all to help you.

4. **"It's a necessity if you're in ministry: how can you minister without your marching orders, without a source of strength, wisdom, and comfort?"** You may not feel like a minister but as a Christian, God will probably give you a ministry of some sort. It may be one-on-one, helping someone in your living unit. It may be leading a small group. Or it may be more up-front, like leading a Young Life Club or serving as the worship leader in your college group. And if you do have a ministry, you need to be equipped. A quiet time helps in that area. God speaks to you through his Word, and he provides wisdom, comfort, and strength. That's what the guys in my group said. I believe them.

5. **"It's a way to better know God, a chance to spend time with him."** Christianity is a relationship, not a religion. To develop any relationship takes some quality time, which a quiet time provides. As the days go by, you'll find you know God better because you've spent time with him. Your relationship will grow and develop, and you'll become more mature in your faith.

6. **"Jesus set the example for quiet times. We should follow our leader."** Jesus told his disciples, "Follow me." If we're sincere about following him, we'll want to do what he said. One of the things he did was to meet with God in times of quiet. He spent a night in prayer alone with God before making the monumental decision of selecting the twelve disciples. And there are several other times in the Bible when he got away to himself at night or in the early morning to be alone with God. If Jesus needed those times, we do too.

7. **"Jesus said, 'I am the bread of life'; we all need spiritual food. Think of a quiet time as**

having breakfast." Physically, we all need to eat. Prolonged fasting leads to death. Spiritually, we all need to eat. A quiet time is mealtime. It's the time when we consume spiritual food and recharge our bodies and spiritual batteries. It's not an option; it's a necessity.

8. **"Suggestion: think of a quiet time not just as an act of obedience or discipline but as an act of love. You are going to meet your friend, your Father, your Savior, your Lord."** Too often we've been bombarded with the notion that having quiet times is a duty and an act of obedience. We do have a duty as a Christian, and we are called to live a life of obedience, but a quiet time is more than that. We've been invited by the Creator and Master of the Cosmos to meet with him. Just the two of us. I've got a great wife. A great Mom and Dad. Fun kids. I don't mind meeting with them. I look forward to it. A quiet time is a "best friend" time. A chance to spend time with Jesus. What a privilege.

So the eight reasons just listed should motivate us to have quiet times. If you're properly motivated, what's next? *What are the key elements to a good quiet time?*

Obviously, the *Bible* is important. A good quiet time involves reading the Word. View the Bible as God's love letter to you. He

wants to impart each day something that will be helpful for your life. Something about your relationship to him. Something about how to live successfully and wisely. God wants to motivate, inform, inspire us. God wants to teach and equip us.

Where do you start in reading the Word? I suggest if you haven't read much of the Bible that you start with a Gospel, maybe Mark or John, and read a chapter a day or several paragraphs a day. After reading a Gospel, it may be fun to read an epistle, then back to another gospel. Later on, get into the Old Testament. Read some Proverbs, Psalms, or some stories from Genesis, Joshua, Judges, Samuel, Ruth, or Esther.

As you read, ask three ques-

Think of prayer simply as talking to a friend who listens and responds because he loves you.

tions. *What does it say here?* In other words, isolate the facts, rephrase what's been said. Then ask yourself: *What does it mean?* Interpret it. And finally, ask the question, *So what?* That is, what difference does it make in your life? How should you apply what you've read? Recently, I finished reading Matthew 1. It's very familiar material to me but as I read the verses that focus on Joseph (verses 18-24), I got a new appreciation for this man (Jesus' earthly father) and for how God uses ordinary people. I realized the working of obedience in this man's life. Joseph listened and did what God asked. On the day I was reading this passage, I was struggling with a couple areas of obedience in my life. What hit me was I needed to be faithful to God in these areas where I'd become a bit slack. So in my prayer time later, I specifically asked for God's power to be obedient — this is how I made practical application of what I had read in the Bible.

After reading Scripture, I would go to *prayer*. Think of prayer simply as talking to a friend who

listens and responds because he loves you. But also consider that you are talking to the Creator of the Cosmos, the Lord of all. Bearing in mind that God is a friend, as well as Lord, should help you find the right balance in your concept of who God is.

One the of the first obstacles to prayer that I face is a wandering mind. Sometimes the first words I say signal my mind to begin remembering all I've left undone the previous day, all I want to do today, all the things I should have said or not said or should say, and so on. My mind wanders. I suggest that you *make your wandering mind a subject of prayer*. If it wanders, pray about the topic of your wanderings. If it's something you need to do like "call home" pray about your home, the call, your family, and then jot down what you need to do on a "to do" list and go back to prayer.

Another concern about prayer is, "What do I pray about? What are the ingredients of prayer?" Personally, I think we make prayer too complicated, too elaborate. Here are some areas you may want to address in prayer. **Praise and Thanksgiving**. Simply thank God for who he is, for what he's done in your life and in the lives of others now and throughout history. **Confession**. We've talked about this in an earlier chapter. Are there some things you need to confess to the Father? Things you haven't already confessed. **Intercession**. That means interceding, intervening on behalf of others. Praying for others' needs. I like to have a prayer list. When I tell someone I'll be praying for them, I like to make sure I do. So I write their name on my list. My mother is a real woman of prayer and has a very long list — so long that she doesn't try to pray for everyone everyday. Instead, she has a Monday list, a Tuesday list, and a list for each day of the week, and she and my dad faithfully pray for the people on each list. When she tells someone, "I've prayed for you every Friday for the last seven months," you know she has. The last area is known as **supplication**. That means praying for your own needs. You know what they are. God knows what they are but he wants us to bring them to him anyway. Nothing is too small or too big for God. Remember that.

The guys in my group also mentioned "body position" when it comes to praying. Some of them have found it helpful to kneel, or to stand with hands upraised, or to sit holding the palms upward in a posture of being ready to receive what God has for you this day. I sometimes pray in those positions but generally my quiet time is at my desk, and I talk to God as I would on the phone or in my office with anyone else.

Another element of a quiet time you may want to consider is *meditating*. Meditating is reflecting, thinking, contemplating. Think about a short passage of Scripture. For example, "The Lord is my shepherd." What does that mean? Think about the words, the concepts. Imagine Jesus coming into your life as a shepherd. What does the good shepherd need to do for you? What do you need to do for the good shepherd? How

can you be a better sheep for the shepherd? Continue to think and meditate. Then as you move through the day, continue your meditation. Or put yourself into a biblical story. If you are reading the story of Jesus meeting Zacchaeus, put yourself in Zacchaeus' place. Imagine climbing the tree, seeing Jesus, hearing him speak to you. Imagine being invited down to spend the mealtime with him. Think what your response would be.

Take some *notes* during your quiet time. Some people call this journaling. Write down what you've studied, what you've learned.I began this process in my senior year in high school over twenty years ago, and it's fun and encouraging to go back over my journals and see how God has faithfully walked with me. You don't have to be super-detailed. Simply jot down what you stud-

ied, what you are learning, and your prayer requests. If you want to write about your day and how God met your needs and how you related to him, that would be good as well.

What happens if you miss your quiet time. If you start and then stall. The guys from the group have a couple of suggestions.

1. **Don't get discouraged.** Everyone misses at one time or another. Satan would love to rob you of the joy of a quiet time by reminding you of how many you've missed. He'd love to discourage you to the point you wouldn't ever want to have another quiet time. Don't worry about it when you miss. Just get going the next day. Having a regular place and a regular time built into your schedule may help you be consistent. That way your quiet time won't be "up for grabs" each day. You won't have to wonder "when?" You'll know.

2. **Don't try to catch up.** If you've been going through a chapter a day and you miss two days, don't try to catch up by reading three chapters. I don't believe God is counting chapters or days. He just wants to spend time with you.

3. **Start the next day**. Just begin again. And don't look at God as the Celestial Policeman who is going to punish you for

the days you've missed. Rather, he's like a loving Father who's been waiting for you and has the feast prepared.

I'd also like to caution you to have a realistic view of quiet times. You may not get a lot out of each one. You may not have much to apply from what you've read. That's okay. Every meal in life is not spectacular. You may not be able to remember what you learned a week later. That's okay. Very few of us remember everything we've eaten in the past week. We do, however, know we've eaten and that our bodies have been nourished. Sometimes you'll get bored. You'll need a change of pace. Here are some suggestions of changes to perk up your quiet times.

1. **Switch Bibles.** Use a different translation for a time. Or get a new Bible. There's something about the smell and feel of a new Bible that gets you excited.

2. **Switch approaches.** You may want to pick up some devotional literature from your Bible bookstore to use for a few weeks. Or you may want to work through a workbook. I've used prayer books sometimes when my prayers seemed a bit flat. Or I've tried just concentrating on a single paragraph on some days. Other periods I've spent time reading longer sections of Scripture to get the flow of the book.

3. **Switch locations.** I've moved from my office at home to the dining room for awhile to have my quiet times. You may want to try a change in scenery too.

A quiet time is vital. Just ask the guys in my group: Jim Allen, Larry Blaine, Dan Larson, Eric Lingren, and Ben Sigman. They almost daily get in personal contact with the most powerful, most wealthy, most wise person in all of creation.

WHAT I'D

If I had it to do over again, I'd watch the grass grow. In college, I mean. In the middle of a concrete city campus. As far as one could see, there was concrete. We walked concrete ramps from the parking garage to the science building; ate our lunch on concrete benches in the concrete park where water spouted from a concrete fish. We soaked up the summer's rays, lying on cement reading our books, and we listened to anti-Vietnam war activists from concrete steps in the forum.

There were several blades of grass on campus one week, but they were only there because some enterprising botanist planted grass in a window box and set it on the sidewalk with a sign that read, "Please stay off the grass." If you wanted real grass, you had to walk due east about eight blocks to the lake — over or under the Dan Ryan Expressway — through an old garment district of the city and across eight lanes of Lake Shore Drive. It was a lot of bother just to see grass. I usually didn't bother. I sat in the concrete wedges called classrooms and conscientiously scribbled notes for five or six hours a day. When class was over I headed for the stacks where I plowed through ancient volumes of English literature. Literature was one of my majors and no matter how much I read, it was never enough.

Then there were my speech courses — speech research labs, speech and media labs, speech recitals, speech projects, speech abstracts, and speech performances to evaluate. I clocked myself from morning till night, crossed off the items one by one on my list of things to do. I met my deadlines, fulfilled my responsibilities, produced grades I could be proud of. Today, twenty-one years later, if you'd ask me, I can not tell you what one of my grades were, nor could I tell you what the grass looks like on the other side of the Dan Ryan Expressway.

I do not live among concrete structures anymore, and grass grows in profusion in my backyard. But I still make my lists, clock myself, and drive to finish my goals. My husband has bought me a hammock that hangs between the patio and the crabapple tree. Now and then I force myself to leave my word processor, retreat to my hammock, stare up into the sky or watch the cardinals eat sunflower seeds from my birdfeeders. Sometimes I feel guilty for wasting time, and some-

times I think that perhaps I'd enjoy my backyard more today if I'd taken an hour now and then in college to emerge from the stacks, cross the expressway, and watch the grass grow along the lakefront. Perhaps it is not too late to learn. But then, maybe it is. I've just typed right through my ten o'clock coffeebreak.

Ruth Senter graduated from Manheim Central High School, Manheim, Pennsylvania, and Moody Bible Institute. She has a B.A. degree in Speech and Communications from the University of Illinois, Chicago Circle Campus. Upon completion of her degree she became production editor for Christian Life *magazine and later returned to Wheaton College where she received a Masters degree in Journalism.*

Ruth is editor of Partnership *magazine and has authored a number of books including* Seasons of Friendship, Startled by Silence, *and* Beyond Safe Places and Easy Answers. *Ruth and her husband Mark have two children: Jori (16) and Nick (12).*

When not lying in her hammock watching the clouds, Ruth is reading a book, antique hunting, or walking along Salt Creek and around the Carol Stream lagoon.

PART THREE

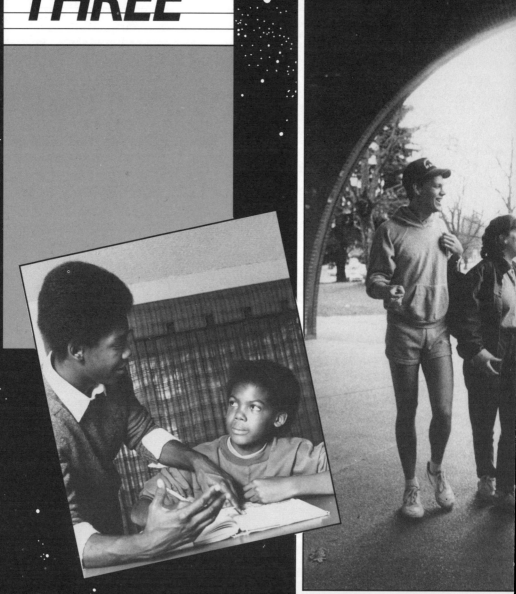

SKILLS

9

How to manage your time

Time is a nonrenewable *resource*. As life goes on, this truth becomes more of a reality: we either use time or we lose it. Time is *valuable* and *irretrievable*. Once it's gone, it's gone. We can't save it. We can't reclaim it.

On the other hand, time is an *equal-opportunity* resource. We may not all have the same talents and gifts but we all have the same amount of time. Twenty-four hours a day; 168 hours a week; 175,200 hours every twenty years.

And because we use time to accomplish everything we do and to be who we are, the management of time is crucial. Successful people who pursue excellence know how to use time. They know how to manage their hours to get the most from the moment. One of the greatest helps to you as you approach your college years is to learn and practice some time-management skills.

So let's look at a dozen time-management ideas and some practical suggestions for making the most of this great resource.

1. **Consider time extremely valuable.** Don't "waste time." Don't "kill time" unless that is what you really want to do with those particular minutes. View time as God's great resource to you. As the Bible says, "Redeem the time." Make it count. Use it,

don't abuse it. (Note: This doesn't mean you shouldn't relax. But we'll talk about that later.)

2. **Don't become a time-management freak.** There is no need to run around with a stopwatch always trying to do three things at once. Showering, shaving, and reading Sports Illustrated all at the same time just won't do. Don't try to talk to your roommate, write a letter, and memorize Russian at once. Relax. Time is valuable but you don't have to become obsessed about it. It's a gift from God, not a curse.

3. **Plan ahead.** There is an old time-management adage, "An hour spent in planning saves three or four in execution," which simply means that by planning, we can maximize our time. We can make each hour count more by thinking ahead about how we want to use it.

This means we need to give ourselves some time to plan. There are several specific ways we can do that. One is to take a half hour or so at the beginning of the week to plan the week ahead. That's called *weekly planning*. When you plan your week, you think about what must be accomplished, what deadlines you must meet, what must be done each day to meet those deadlines. As you plan, make sure you give yourself time for recreation as well

as work. Plan for balance and wholeness in your life. (We'll talk more about that in chapter 15.)

That same strategy should be used for *daily planning*. Before you go to bed, think about the next day. What needs to be done? What errands need to be run? Who do you want to see? What do you need to study? Then think through a schedule for that day so you can maximize your hours.

A final way to plan is what I call *project planning*. Whenever you have a project, a term paper, anything that involves more than one task, think it through in advance. Isolate the steps you'll have to take to complete it. What should be done first, second, and so on? By planning you don't waste as much energy running from one task to another, and you

know the order in which you must do each step.

So plan ahead. An hour in planning does save three or four hours in execution. And remember when you plan, *write it down*. Getting those plans on paper helps crystallize your thinking and helps you to remember what you've planned.

4. **As you plan, think in terms of priorities.** Prioritizing means that you simply compare your goals and activities and assign value to them. You decide what is most important, second in importance, third in importance, and so on. For example, if you are a college freshman and have listed the follow activities for the day, "finish English paper, read 40 pages in history text, play racquetball with Jon, clean desk, write home," you would decide first what was the most important to do. If the English paper was worth half your grade for the semester and if you were an English major and if the paper was due the next day, the paper would probably take top billing. Next in line might be writing home. Especially if you hadn't written all quarter, and you were in desperate need of money!

Some people, when they prioritize, think in terms of A, B, and C priorities, with A items being of utmost importance, followed by B and C. Some people even go to the extreme of prioritizing their A, B, and C priorities. If you have two A priorities for the day, you might label the most important A-1, the next A-2.

5. **Act on your priorities.** If you went to the trouble, time, and effort to plan your day and prioritize your activities, then it makes sense to follow through. Begin with your top priority and continue down the list.

One of the easiest ways to focus on priorities is to have a simple "To Do" list. Here's an example.

---

1. Write English paper.
2. Write home.
3. Play racquetball with Jon.
4. Read 40 pages of history.
5. Clean desk.

When you finish number one (your highest priority item), check it off. This gives you a sense of accomplishment and a little drive to do the next item. If you don't finish everything on your list, save it for the next day. But don't make what you've left undone today as the number one priority for tomorrow unless after planning, you've decided it deserves to be number one. For instance, let's suppose as you plan for the next day, you realize the number one priority is an event you've had on your schedule for some time. Your college church group is going on an all-day white water rafting trip, and you're fired up about it. That's still number one. You'd like to get in some of the history reading that night but you're sure you can live with the messy desk at least another day. So your "To Do" list for tomorrow would look like this.

---

1. Go on white water rafting trip (remember to bring lunch and wetsuit).
2. Read 40 pages of history.
3. Clean desk.

One word of caution. Sometime soon the history reading and the messy desk will probably rise to the top of the list. You can't keep procrastinating on your history anymore than you could delay writing the English paper. And the messy desk, over time, will cause you to waste time as you frantically dig through the rubble trying to find assignments or paper clips. Orderliness then (if not carried to extreme) is a time-management help. I speak with authority. I've been waging war with my messy desk for years and still haven't won consistently!

6. **Know yourself.** That doesn't sound much like a time-management principle, does it? But it is. Two ways in particular are helpful in knowing yourself. The first is, *know your prime time*. Prime time is the time when you function best. The time when you're most alert, have the most energy, and are best able to handle pressure. For me, I'm a morning person. But I've known others who were regular night owls. They worked best when everyone else is asleep.

When is your prime time? Get to those important things during that time. Because I'm a morning person, I take advantage of my energy to accomplish my top priority items in the first hours of the day. If you're a morning person too, you might try scheduling your classes so your most difficult ones are in the morning. Have your Bible study in the morning as well. Give God the

best of your day.

Know, too, how much *sleep* you need. Not everyone needs an equal amount of sleep. Get what you need, not what your friends get by on. You need sleep for health and energy. Life is a marathon. There will be times when you have to sprint and may have to go without needed sleep but know how much you usually need and get it. The principle here: know your prime time and your sleep time.

7. **Give yourself good chunks of time for A priorities.** Sometimes you can do things in little bits and pieces of time. But on the really important items where you need to concentrate, give yourself chunks of time, hours of time to work on a project. If I tried to write a book in five-minute spurts, I'd be in trouble. I'd lose my train of thought, my powers of concentration. So I reserve *hours* when I can write. And I try to reserve those hours when I'm at my best (my prime time) and when I am less likely to be interrupted. The same should work for you.

8. **Divide and conquer tasks.** Break the big projects down into small-sized bites. For instance, if you're doing a term paper, break this large task into smaller tasks, like choosing a topic, finding seven good reference books, skimming each one for material,

checking the periodicals, making an outline of the paper, building a bibliography, and writing the introduction. A term paper will not overwhelm you if you use the divide and conquer method. And while you're dividing, come up with some "instant tasks" — tasks that can be done in five minutes or less. Then, when you only have a few minutes but would still like to be working on your top priority, you can read an article from a periodical or begin to build your bibliography or start on an outline.

9. **Have a getaway place when you need to hide out and get things done or need to be alone.** I'm on the staff of a church

that sits on the corner of a major university. At the university, there are dozens of good places to study. But I know some students who have a hideout at our church. Some use the third floor of our Christian education building where the preschool kids meet on Sunday morning. For most of the week and especially at night, these rooms are vacant. Sitting at miniature tables by themselves are students who are in "hiding." Their friends don't know where they are. They won't be inter-rupted. It's "their place." Find a place where you can get away alone when the pressure is intense and when you need privacy.

10. **Utilize waiting time.** All of us have to wait. At the grocery store. In registration lines. At the dentist. Have something to do while you wait so you can maximize that time. In the past, I've carried *TIME* magazine with me and read it while I wait. At other times, I've kept postcards in my back pocket, already addressed and stamped, so whenever I had

Find a place where you can get away alone when the pressure is intense and when you need privacy.

to wait, I'd pull out a card and write a quick note to a friend. Instant correspondence. I also use waiting time to pray for people.

11. **Write a note to yourself when an interruption occurs.** Let's suppose you are working on that English paper we talked about before. You're in your room and, all of a sudden, your buddy comes charging in with some great news. Before you stop to give him your full attention, write a note to yourself on what you're going to do next on the paper. You don't know how long your friend will be there. Thirty seconds. Thirty minutes. Three hours. You can't afford to lose your next thought on that paper. Write it down. Then when he leaves, you can look at your note, regain your thoughts, and move on. It saves time and frustration.

12. **When in doubt, ask yourself a question: what's the best use of my time now?** Ask yourself this question if you happen to be waiting or when you've finished one project and are ready for the next. Or when praying, ask God that question. What's the best use of my time now? This question is always a winner in trying to figure out what to do next.

In conclusion, let me say that there are literally hundreds of books and seminars on managing time. You can become an absolute obsessive-compulsive person if you get too caught up in saving minutes and making the most of your time. So relax. Realize time is valuable and irretrievable but that God loves you and wants you to live a balanced life.

In the next chapter on how to study, we'll discuss some other time-management helps.

WHAT I'D

I would study more about the fine arts to better understand my own culture.

I would travel more to become aware of the world in which I live.

I would take a speed reading course to sharpen both reading and comprehension skills.

I would not be so critical of fellow students and faculty members or expect them to attain standards I had set for them.

I would spend more time with adults who had proven effective in my chosen field.

I would not sever my family ties quite so completely that I would need to rebuild those relationships later on.

I would take more courses in business and finance so as not to have learned so many financial lessons the hard way.

BUT...

I would be just as involved in extracurricular activities as I was then, for in them I learned to prioritize my time.

I would maintain the same high standards and qualities for myself and the women I dated.

I would set my personal goals just as clearly on serving the Lord in every aspect of life.

I would still attend Bible school before completing my college education even though it meant squeezing my four years of college into seven years.

I would still be involved in Christian ministries outside the college in order to keep my feet in the real world.

Mark Senter graduated from Hampden Du Bose Academy, Moody Bible Institute, the University of Illinois (Chicago Circle), and Trinity Evangelical Divinity School.

He is currently a Ph.D. candidate at Loyola University in Chicago.

Mark has served both as a youth pastor and associate pastor in several churches and is now assistant professor of Christian education at Trinity Evangelical Divinity School.

10

How to study

There are few secrets to becoming a good student. The key to studying involves a little skill and a lot of hard work. But there are some basic fundamentals that will be helpful to you as you hit the big time when the academic work load intensifies. This chapter is designed to help you study "smart," not just "hard and long."

Here are a few important suggestions on how you can become a better student.

The first is obvious. **Go to class**. Go to class everyday. Your peers and roommates may not set a good example in this area but go to class anyhow. The college experience is too short to get into the habit of missing classes on a regular basis. Besides, the benefits for going to class daily are worth the effort.

• Going to class establishes credibility. Not only does it prove to the professor and to your classmates that you are a serious student but it also disciplines you to be consistent and diligent. This, you'll need when you begin your first post-college job.

• Sometimes bonus points are awarded for attendance. And most of us need all the points we can get.

• No matter how dumb the prof seems, every now and then something he/she says will be impor-

tant and will likely appear on the exam. You don't want to be taken by surprise. A friend of mine had this to say about class attendance, "Even if I knew the class was going to be a sleeper, I would go anyway and write a letter or study other materials and listen just in case something happened."

• Pop quizzes sometimes occur. A score of "zero" because you were sleeping in is hard to take.

• You paid for the class (or at least your parents did). You might as well get your money's worth.

• Going to class is part of good stewardship of time, money, and God's gift to us of this opportunity for an education.

Sure there are times when you'll miss a class. But when you know you have to miss class, at least make sure a friend will take quality notes for you. Depending on the size of the class, you may want to talk to the prof in advance. It will show you have enough interest to get the assignments and any information the professor had planned to give the students. Often special arrangements can be made for you.

Second, **take notes in class**. It's a good idea to have an individual notebook for each class or a three-ring binder with dividers to record notes in each class. Class notes will help you in reviewing for tests, in recalling the

material, and in staying awake when the lecture gets dull. You will need to develop a good system for taking notes. Don't try taking down everything the professor says, just the key points. It's also helpful as you write to leave about a fourth of your page vacant for extra notations later, as on the example below. Sometimes a prof may come back to a topic

Sample page of classroom notes

Notes on the left side of the page.

Blank space on the right for additional comments later.

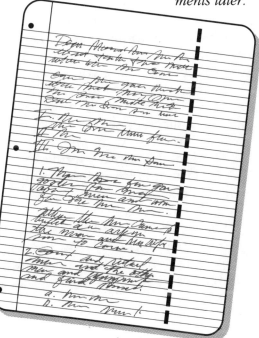

already covered, and you'll want the room for the additional comments. Or as you study for a test, you may want to make your own notes in the extra space next to a class note. One thing you should keep in mind — you may not be a great note taker just starting out in your college experience but you will improve with time.

Third, **make some friends in each class**. It helps to have study partners and someone to exchange notes with.

Fourth, **try to get to know the professor personally**. It will help in the long run if he or she recognizes your face and name. When a good relationship is formed, it will be easier to get one-on-one assistance when you need it. Besides, most profs are interesting people, and part of the college experience is meeting and interacting with new people.

Fifth, **if you need extra assistance outside the classroom, find out whether a tutor is available**. Work at understanding the material. If you don't understand something, ask questions of profs, friends, fellow students, or tutors. Make sure you take advantage of every resource available to you in understanding the material.

Sixth, **choose your classes carefully each quarter or semester**. As you put together your course load, consider your habits and lifestyle. If you are a morning person and function best in the morning, take your most difficult classes in the morning and study in the morning as well. Take advantage of the time when you're at your best. If you're a late-nighter, try staying away from early morning classes. If you are a person who gets tired after lunch, avoid taking any early afternoon classes. Of course, it is not always possible to fit your classes to your awake/sleep cycle.

Also try to even out your class load. For instance, if you're taking three classes, select two that are difficult and one, not so difficult. Pace yourself. Also consider the other activities you are involved in during the term. If you're in a dramatic production or playing on the football team, you'll want to make your fall schedule as light as possible. Then during winter quarter, when the snow is three feet deep, you can schedule your hardest load. In spring (when flowers are blooming, birds are singing, and bees, buzzing) you might take a medium load and take advantage of the season.

Seventh, **block out time for studying**. You'll need to schedule your study time. Begin by constructing a schedule like the one at the right. First, write in your set appointments and activities, including your quiet time with God, your scheduled classes, your

fellowship meetings, intramural sports, work, and so on. Then write down study times for each class. A good rule of thumb is to allot two hours of study time for every one hour of class. If you're taking a five-hour English Literature class, you'll need to budget ten hours of study per week. You might also try to work into your schedule a day to take off from studying. On Sundays, I used to postpone studying until after our

	M	T	W	Th	F	Sa	Su
7	Quiet Time	QT	QT	QT	QT		
8	Psych 101	Psych 101	Psych 101	Psych 101	Psych 101		Worship
9	Eng 102		Eng 102		Eng 102		
10	Study Eng.		Study Eng.	Art 103	Study Eng.		
11	"	Art 103	"		"		
12	Lunch	Lunch	Lunch	Lunch	Lunch		
1							
2	Workout	WO	WO	WO	WO		
3	Psych Lab		Study	Study	Study	Study	
4	"		"	"	"	"	
5	"		"	Dinner	Dinner	Dinner	
6	Dinner	Dinner	History 140		History 140		
7			"		"		
8		Study	TV	Study	Rec. Reading	Study	
9	Study	"	"	"	"		
10	"						

91

college youth group met on Sunday nights; it made Sundays more relaxed and a day I could look forward to. As you plan your study times, give yourself *chunks* of time, not *bits* of time. Don't try to study in fifteen-minute blocks. Get in an hour or more of study time.

Eighth, **take a break**. In a study block of several hours, take a five-to-ten-minute break every hour to walk around, visit with friends, or go to the restroom. This is not wasting time. The break helps you

maximize the rest of your study time by allowing you to clear your head, to "wake up," before you move on to your next section of work. And it gives you something to look forward to. A break tells you, "I have some relief in sight. This is not a death march, a prison camp. I get a break in just fifty minutes." But one word of caution — don't study for ten minutes and break for fifty! Be disciplined, and don't abuse your break.

Ninth, **study over an extended period of time**. Plan ahead. Waiting until the night before the test to do your reading and review will not work. The night before the test should serve strictly as a review time, not as a cram time. It is not a time to begin learning the basic concepts of the course. Cramming causes anxiety and sends you into your test with little sleep. And you'll simply not be at your best.

So what are the alternatives to cramming? Regular study. Following the schedule you developed. Regular studying means determining at the start of the quarter or semester how many pages per day or week you'll have to read. For example, if your Russian history course requires 2500 pages of reading and you're on a ten week quarter, you'll have to read 250 pages a week or approximately 50

Dad saw your report card.

pages a day (with two days a week left over to take a break from Russian history). Each day, check yourself. Are you ahead or behind in your reading? If you keep pace, on the night before the midterm, you won't have to take time reading lots of material. You'll simply be able to review. It beats cramming!

Tenth, **find a place to study**. Be honest with yourself about the kind of place where you'll be able to study best. Some people find that a place too quiet is distracting, and they study best in a lively dormitory. Others need a secluded spot, like the library. Some students prefer a coffee shop setting. College campuses often have interesting nooks and crannies where studying can be done. Figure out under what conditions you are most effective in your studying and find that place.

Eleventh, **be ready when you get to your place of study**. Know what subject you'll be studying, have the right books, papers, equipment (calculators, pencils, graph paper) with you. Then plunge in. Don't waste time "getting ready." Get on with it.

Twelfth, **make notes in your textbook or underline key concepts**. The emphasis is on *key*. Don't underline everything, just enough to help you as you prepare for a test.

Thirteenth, **use index cards to write down key concepts, formulas, and other ideas**. The index cards will be helpful when you review, and they are handy to read over while walking through campus, eating lunch, waiting in a line, or getting ready for bed.

Now let's talk about taking a test.

Fourteenth, **prepare for tests, but don't cram**. Review several days in advance and go over key concepts the night before. Try to get a good night's sleep so you're fresh the next day. Review briefly in the morning before the test. Ask God to give you recall and peace — then march in with confidence, and give it your best shot.

Fifteenth, **be ready when you arrive to take the test**. Have your pencils (extra ones), blue book (if necessary), erasers, rulers, calculators, or whatever

93

back to those questions you skipped. If you don't have time to do them all, at least circle an answer. You may hit a correct answer by chance, and it is a documented fact that the answer (c) is the most often correct multiple-choice answer. At any rate, do not leave questions blank. Blank items are always zero.

Seventeenth, **if you have time, critically review your test upon completion**. Especially when it comes to essay questions. Often blunders, such as incorrect spelling or bad grammar, are a result of reading too fast or your general anxiety. If you're struggling over a multiple-choice or true-false question in your review, go with your first answer.

Eighteenth, **learn from your mistakes**. It's easy to "blow it off" when you don't do well on a test, but don't. Figure out what went wrong. Make the effort to become a better test taker.

Here are some suggestions to consider when it comes to writing papers.

Nineteenth, **start early**. Know the assignment (the deadline, the number of words or pages, and so on.) Decide on a topic. Then give yourself some time to mull over the topic, to think about it, before you begin researching it. If you begin the paper a day before it's due, you haven't allowed yourself

you'll need with you. You'll have enough to be concerned about without having to search for a pencil at the last minute.

Sixteenth, **look the test over before you write anything**. Often tests are designed with certain questions carrying the most weight. Maximum points are often listed for each section of the test. Bring a watch or sit where you can see a clock so that you can budget your time, giving more time to the questions worth the most points. For example, you might skip over the multiple-choice and true-false questions on a test and begin the maximum-point essay questions first. Then before the time is up, you can go

The night before the test should serve strictly as a review time, not as a cram time. It is not a time to begin learning the basic concepts of the course.

---

time to give your work any thought.

Twentieth, **do the basic research**. Learn how to use the library, the card catalog, and the Reader's Guide to Periodicals. Use note cards. Note references. Develop your bibliography as you go along.

Twenty-first, **outline your paper first**. What do you want to say?

Twenty-second, **write a rough draft based on your outline**. Organize the rough draft by forming sentences from your outline.

Twenty-third, **after the rough draft is complete, critique your work**. It is helpful to get some distance from your paper; for a day or at least three hours or more, walk away from it. Then come back and critically read the paper, looking for errors — illogical thought sequences, points that need clarification, weak organization, or other weaknesses.

Twenty-fourth, **write the next draft and repeat step twenty-three**.

Twenty-fifth, **write the final draft and type it well**. Neatness does count with most profs.

These ideas have been used by many conscientious students who wanted to benefit the most from their college experience. My hope is you'll combine these smart approaches with some hard work to discover that your study hours will be effective and beneficial.

There's a tendency on the part of many graduating high-school seniors to overestimate the difficulty of college. You may have heard horror stories about how some profs deliberately try to get students to flunk out, how high-school honor students fail their college courses. The truth is that, though college is more difficult than high school, if you have good work habits and know how to study, you'll do well and you'll succeed. I have confidence in your ability. Follow these principles and enjoy the books!

WHAT I'D

Rosie Weary was born into a family of ten children — seven girls and three boys. She graduated from New Hymn High School in Pinola, Mississippi, and Los Angeles Baptist College. She and her husband, Dolphus, have three children and direct the work of Mendenhall Ministries in Mendenhall, Mississippi.

I can remember so well those years in junior high and high school, trying so desperately to be part of the "in crowd." At the time, it seemed the place to be. However, I realized much later it was not being part of the "in crowd" that gave me worth and a sense of importance, but what was inside of me. How I perceived myself and how God perceived me was what really counted. Had I learned to like myself and had I realized God had made me a unique and special person, I would have spared myself all the futile efforts to be "in."

Looking back to my high-school years, I realize I failed to take advantage of the educational system, which made college a real challenge and struggle for me. I did well in high school scholastically, but I didn't take advantage of everything available to me — the study periods and library — which would have helped me be better equipped for college. When I failed to get an understanding of a particular subject or problem, I was too embarrassed to ask the teacher to explain the material again. That was one of my greatest mis-

takes. I didn't always perform at my peak as a result.

I went from Mississippi to Los Angeles for college. Coming from the South where the dialect is so different from that of the West, I often found it hard to understand my instructors. And because I wouldn't ask questions, I didn't always understand the assignments. If I had to do it over again, I would ask questions until I got a real grasp of the material.

I would also seek to find out what field or professions had the greatest job opportunities and would have gained a skill in one of these areas so that I would be more marketable. Obtaining a degree in an area where there are limited jobs available is not planning for success.

I would also ask someone to give me pointers on good note taking and study habits. I would try to get a cassette recorder to take to class with me to enhance my note taking. Staying aware of political issues would be a high priority for me, as well as being more verbal in classes. I would let people see the real me more, not be inhibited because of how I think people feel about me.

11

How to choose a career

"Choosing a career is one of the most important decisions you'll ever make."

Have you ever heard this statement before? It's true. The decision of what your vocation will be is critical. You want to be in a place where you feel your gifts are being used, where you're making a contribution, and where you are adequately rewarded for the time, energy and skill invested.

But it's also a statement that can be misleading for some. The word "career" sounds as if you choose one field or one occupation in life and remain with it forever. That's not true for many.

I, for instance, have been a writer, a pastor, a businessman, a publisher, a magazine editor, and a consultant. Now this may be unusual, and yet I have friends who have had similar experiences. Career for us isn't cut and dried. Perhaps you're also more of a generalist than a specialist, and God might use you in a variety of fields. You may start in one area and switch to another before you retire from vocational pursuits.

Others, however, will choose one field and stay in it. I've known electrical engineers who enter the field and stay. Or medical doctors, ministers, and teachers who have remained in their chosen profession a lifetime.

What I'd like to do in this chapter is help you choose a career and at the same time, help you relax about your decision. Whether you stay in a field for years, or like me, switch around once in a while, you can know God will use you significantly wherever you are.

Intercristo is an organization in Seattle, Washington (P.O. Box 33487, Seattle, 98133) that call themselves, "The Christian Career Specialists." And they are. They help Christians prepare for careers, and they help some choose "Christian careers," that is, full-time careers in Christian organizations. Recently, Intercristo published a wonderful career kit that includes cassette tapes and booklets designed to help people make an intelligent career choice.

As we think about careers, I'd like to highlight three principles the Intercristo people feel are necessary in understanding God's view of work.

The first principle is *expression*. God expects you to invest your life in work that expresses your abilities. It's okay to enjoy your work! That's part of God's plan for you. Some questions you might ask yourself as you are wondering about your abilities and how best to express them include:

1. What is the ongoing force or desire that drives me?

2. What skills do I possess, and how do I use them?

3. Am I best equipped to work with people, numbers, data, ideas?

4. What circumstances and environment bring out the best work in me?

5. How would I describe my "operating relationships" with others? Am I independent? A team player? Am I the president or supervisor type?

Sometimes you can answer those questions on your own. Or you may want to look into some vocational testing, which many colleges and universities provide. Or perhaps you have a friend who knows you well. Maybe your parents can provide some insight into your abilities and capabilities.

Better yet, a combination of parents, friends, and testing will be helpful in realizing the career that's best for you.

A second principle is *provision*. God expects you to invest your life in work that provides for your needs. As Paul wrote to Timothy (1 Timothy 5:8), "If anyone does not provide for his relatives, and especially for his immediate family, he has denied the faith and is worse than an unbeliever." Your work is to provide not only for your personal needs, but for the needs of those for whom God holds you responsible. Paul underscores this fact in 2 Thessalonians 3:6-12.

The Intercristo writers list four guidelines under the provision principle.

1. *Expect your work to provide for your needs, not your wants.* Even though we live in a materialistic world where advertisers work to increase our wants, the basic needs of life are few: food, shelter, clothing. Christ may call you into a career with lower earnings than some other career, but he will take care of your needs.

2. *Don't underestimate your needs.* God expects your work to be a means of providing for your needs, not a way to slip into poverty.

3. *Provision is not limited to a paycheck.* Provision is measured not only by pay but also by quality of life. It should provide important intangibles, like time for family and friends, and a sense of personal achievement.

4. *Your obligation to provide for others grows right along with your other responsibilities.* If you choose to marry and have children your responsibilities to provide also increase.

Principle number three is *mission*. God expects you to invest your life in work that furthers his kingdom on earth. As Paul wrote to the Corinthian church, "Therefore, my dear brothers, stand firm. Let nothing move you. Always give yourselves fully to the work of the Lord, because you know that your labor in the Lord is not in vain" (1 Corinthians 15:58).

But what exactly is God's mission? Here's how Intercristo describes it: "God intends to draw all those who've never heard of his love to himself. God intends to feed the hungry, restore sight to the blind, and bring wholeness to the broken. God intends to bring justice to the poor, reconciliation to the divided, and peace to those in conflict. God intends that the good news be preached and proclaimed to all nations. God intends that people of every tribe, language, and nation will learn that the Lamb of God, Jesus, has purchased their salvation with his blood. God intends that every stronghold of Satan will be penetrated and shattered with his light and love."

My good friend, Tony Campolo, talks about how we are to be a part of God's mission. Here's what he says in his books and in the speeches he delivers across the country: "I want to make this as clear as I know: I want to emphatically assert that Jesus desperately wants you to allow him to work through you to begin to change his world into the world he wills for it to be."

With an understanding of God's purpose on earth in mind, what are some specific aspects of this mission, and how does it apply to us?

1. *God's work is love in action.* In Matthew 22:37-40, three kinds of love are discussed — loving God, loving self, and loving others. The question becomes then just how specifically are we putting love into action?

2. *God's work is lived out in relationships.* It's people, not programs, that really count. Sure, God often works through programs, but it's people in contact with people that ultimately makes a difference. He wants to touch people through you.

3. *God's work is loving the whole person.* God's concern is not just with the spiritual side of people, or just the physical, or even the emotional or psychological or mental. His concern is the whole person, and our ministry should be to the whole person too.

4. *God's work is word and deed.* The balance of word and deed characterized the early church. And God's purpose is still carried out by what we say and by what we do.

5. *God's work is loving the whole world, beginning where you are.* In the words of author and activist Charles Colson, "The believer's ministry is being Christ's person right where he or she is, in the marketplace or the home, every moment of the day. This is the very nature of loving God."

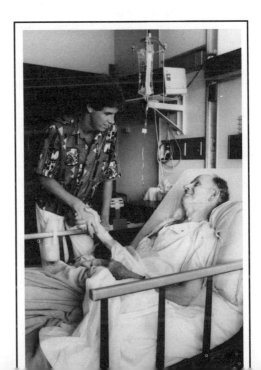

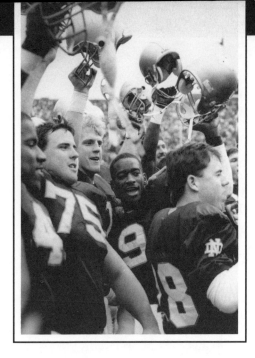

6. *God's work is full time whether you are in full-time Christian work or in the secular arena.* "Every Christian is already in full-time Christian work," according to the Intercristo people and according to the Bible.

7. *God's work is empowered by the Holy Spirit.* "I am the vine; you are the branches ...; apart from me you can do nothing" (John 15:5). "The Spirit of the Lord is on me, because he has anointed me..." (Luke 4:18). When we become a believer the Holy Spirit comes to indwell us. Fulfilling God's mission through work means relying on the power of his spirit, not just on our own effort.

8. *God's work is your work.* God's work is not done by the clergy or by Christian organizations; it's done by all of us.

How can you discover God's work for you? Intercristo gives four suggestions:

1. **Look up!** Pray. Read the Word. Ask the Lord.

2. **Look around!** See the needs of the world. Use them as clues in helping you determine what it is you can do.

3. **Look in!** Look at your heart. What unique experiences have sensitized you to work in the world? Maybe you were raised in a foreign land and have a unique understanding of the people there and know the language. Perhaps you can be involved with people of that nationality in your home country, or maybe you can make a difference for Christ by taking a job overseas.

4. **Look at your talents.** By assessing your skills and talents, you can decide how best to maximize them while addressing the needs of others.

I appreciate Intercristo's work in these areas, and I would encourage you to contact them if you need further study. Check out the career kit too. Your pastor or youth director might have access to one.

Now with these broad principles in mind, let's turn to some more specifics about how to determine the right career choice for you.

Your initial consideration should be what it is you actually *enjoy doing.* What are you really interested in? The next step is to determine if you will need *further education and training*. Do you need to go to college to pursue what you want to do? Many career goals can be achieved outside college. However, don't look at the college experience as simply a vocational training ground. College can prove beneficial beyond vocational preparation; it is a chance to wrestle with some critical issues, an opportunity to develop friendships.

If you do decide college is the ticket, then you need to ask yourself which *major field of study* will put you in a position to learn the appropriate skills. Now that's fairly simple —*if* you know what you want to do. But the reality is that few of us really know for sure what we want to do when we enter college. Or if we know what we want to do, the decision may change as we gain new information.

When I started college, I wanted to be a psychiatrist. I knew that would involve medical school and years of internships and residency. But that was all right with me. I had done well in chemistry, physics, and biology in high school although none of those subjects were particularly favorites of mine. I had loved the one psychology course I took in high school, which had really

turned me on to the idea of psychiatry. I liked people and enjoyed listening to them. And I was a "rescuer," a "problem solver." I thought those traits would make a good psychiatrist. So off I went to college.

I quickly discovered that pre-med students don't take a *little* chem and biology. They take a ton of it, and that wasn't for me. I suppose I could have persevered, but I didn't want to. So I kept my original major, psychology, but modified my career goals. I wanted to be a psychologist instead.

In my junior year, I was approached by a professor who had heard of a church needing a part-time youth director. He asked me

It's not that I don't respect your mother's opinion, but do you have any other references?

if I would be interested. I had been involved in church functions most of my life; I had worked as a recreation director in the summers; and I had taken a few Christian education courses. My professor thought I was qualified. Maybe I was, but my primary motivation in taking the job was I needed the money! Somehow God used my need and my talents, and I became a youth director while attending college. I enjoyed the job and the students and had a wonderful time. I also began to discover some personal ministry gifts. I realized I enjoyed

teaching, preaching, counseling, and encouraging and motivating people.

So when I graduated from college I had several options. The church offered me a full-time position as youth director, so I could have continued in that work. I was also considering attending either seminary or graduate school in psychology. Again, through circumstances and conscious decisions, I chose to do further studies in psychology. I received a teaching assistantship and headed for grad school. I did well scholastically that first quarter, but I hated it. Grad school wasn't for me. At least not this graduate program; it's emphasis was heavy on behavioral psychology and scholastic research, and I felt it just wasn't what I wanted to do. New information had come into play in my career pursuits. I decided to leave graduate school and continue in Christian youth work.

As I mentioned earlier in this chapter, I've had several different jobs in my career. Youth work led me to a position of director of Christian education at First Presbyterian Church in San Diego. While in San Diego, I met two youth workers, Wayne Rice and Mike Yaconelli, who had started a company to provide resources and services for youth workers nationally. I joined forces with them in what turned out to be a publishing, seminar, and convention business. This, in turn, led me into writing and editing, which then led me into doing consulting work, and which finally led me back into the church. My "career" has, therefore, been circuitous. But enriching and meaningful. I believe God has allowed me *expression, provision* and *mission.* And I'm grateful.

So what happens if *you* don't know what to do or you're not sure? I asked my friend and co-worker, Rod Handley, whom I

mentioned in a previous chapter, this question. You may remember he's the C.P.A. who left a prestigious accounting firm to work with students. As a guy who faithfully pursued one career before making a major career switch, Rod offers two options for those who aren't sure what to do.

1. **Don't go to school.** Get a job and keep your eyes open. It's not bad to wait a year or two to figure out what you want to do. And being in the work force might be very good for you.

2. **Go to school.** But concentrate on the basics. Talk to professors, roommates, friends, upperclassmen. By taking basic classes, you won't lose the credits if you

end up changing your career plans and your major.

As you go about choosing a career, here are some other important questions to ask yourself.

1. **Who's influencing my choice?**

• Is your choice simply based on following in the footsteps of your parents or an older brother or sister? Maybe you have always liked the field your Mom is in. Perhaps you have an opportunity to take over the family business when you graduate. Or maybe you and your older sister have similar gifts, and you'd like to pursue what she has pursued. Perhaps following in your brother's tracks might be wise under certain circumstances. But if you're just following someone to avoid working out your own direction, you may want to rethink your goals.

• Is your choice based on something you think you "should do" rather than something you'd like to do? Maybe you think you should go into the pastoral ministry because the church needs pastors, and people need to hear the gospel. And yet the idea of being a pastor is a "face tightener" for you. It's an "ought to do" instead of a "want to do." Bruce Larson, my friend, my boss and my senior pastor, suggests not going into the ministry if there's anything else you can do or want to do. You should enjoy what you're doing. If you are motivated only by what you think you should do, people will sense it, and you'll eventually become discontented in your work. After several years of not working in a church, I'm back on a church staff with Bruce and some other wonderful colleagues. I'm having the time of my life not because I'm doing something I think I should or ought to do, but because I enjoy working with students.

• Are your peers and culture influencing your choice? Are you motivated by what your friends think? If everyone is going for the business degree because that's supposedly the ticket to a job, do you feel reluctant pursuing an elementary teaching certificate?

2. **What's influencing my choice?**

Is it fame, fortune, security? If so, is that really what you want to base your life on? Or is it stewardship of your gifts, a desire to be obedient to Christ whatever the amount of the paycheck?

3. **Finally, will this career choice help me fulfill my dreams to make a difference in the world?**

Pray about this important choice. Talk to God. Talk to friends, professors, family members who know you. Talk to others in the fields in which you're interested. Get as much information as possible. Be open, be willing to listen, and be "interruptible."

Count the costs. What will this career cost you in preparation? Are you willing to go the distance? To hang in there? Remember that God never wastes an experience. If you should happen to invest a few years in preparing for one career and then change your mind, God will still use those years and experiences you might otherwise have labeled "futile."

Once you do, in fact, take a job and begin a career, don't give up too early. The first six months on any job is a time of adaptation. You are learning to organize your time, to relate to peers and others in authority. You are learning how to delegate and accept more responsibility. That won't be easy. So don't make a hasty decision to get out before you've had a chance to know for sure if you've made the right choice.

Choosing a career is an important decisions, but God walks with you and works with you. So enjoy the adventure of choosing and preparing for a career, and maybe even of changing careers down the road.

WHAT I'D

David Tyner graduated from Father Judge High School in Philadelphia. Upon graduation, he joined the United States Air Force where he served for eight and a half years. He now is president of Tyner and Associates, Inc., a commercial insurance agency.

My graduation day looms as clear in my mind as if it were yesterday. I recall the exhilaration I had going to the graduation ceremonies. "Thank God, it's over," I remember thinking. But the real adventure was just beginning.

Even though I was graduating from a Catholic high school and had had religious instruction all through my school years, God really was not a conscious part of my life, until later. God was not real for me; he was a foggy perception, a concept, someone I prayed to real hard when I was in deep trouble.

I recall my mother asking me about college on my graduation day. But it was too late; I wanted *out* of school, and I had already made my plans. I could finally get out into the world to create my own destiny, and I was *very* determined to make something of myself. Life had been difficult up to that point, extremely disappointing, and unhappy. My parents had been divorced since I was in the third grade, and I wanted to free myself from the racial hatred I had felt in school. Being one of only a few blacks in an overwhelmingly Irish, German, Polish, American high school, I wanted to free myself from the narrow thinking of both blacks and whites, of teachers, adults, and of other young people. I just knew there had to be a better opportunity for me away from Philadelphia, away from the disappointment, strife, and bitterness I had experienced growing up. So I decided I wanted to join the Air Force, travel, see new faces and places.

Joining the U.S. Air Force right out of high school was the single best thing I could have done for myself. I wouldn't change that. It immediately put me in touch with new disciplines, organization, and a map for my future. It was a great place to start. But I had so much to learn. So much to learn about following instructions *exactly,* and about people. What a shock to meet white southerners with their drawl. Were they really as bad as I had read and heard? I had contact with blacks from Detroit, Chicago, Dallas, Birmingham. Wow! And I met Hispanics and Latin Americans. I remember always asking different guys about what it was like where they grew up.

The Air Force matured me, taught me a skill, took me to my first duty station up on Cape Cod. Four years later, I was in Vietnam. I learned much in a short period of time. After the war, I transferred to Japan. And after four years there, I took a discharge overseas to Japan and went into business with about a dozen friends of mine. I entered the arena of foreign trade and finance and learned my craft of sales and marketing.

If I had it to do all over again, I would have loved to have learned to find *balance* in life. A spiritual, physical, mental balance. I would have loved to have understood the importance of having the Lord as a friend and resource. I would want to know more about how to choose friends and avoid bad ones. I had to learn so many things the hard way. A painful experience, not recommended.

I would suggest that young people not be in a hurry to get married. Choosing a life's partner is a critical decision. Find out about yourself. Test yourself in terms of challenges and adventures. Learn to love the Lord, to make friends with him. Love God with all your heart, love your fellow man, love yourself. Learn how to be an effective communicator, to speak, write, and convey your message. Don't be concerned with status, build your strength from within, and you won't have to worry about what people think.

12

How to choose a life partner

So you want to get married someday. That's a great idea! God has designed us for relationships and wants us to enjoy the fantastic relationship we can have with a person to whom we are committed in marriage.

I'm glad I'm married. I love my wife and family. And it's my hope for you that you'll be able to enjoy marriage and family as much as I do.

But maybe you're reluctant to even think about marriage. You've seen plenty of marriages fail. Maybe you've watched your own parents' marriage go down in flames. You've seen more mediocre marriages than good ones. You want to marry, but you want to marry well. How do you choose a life partner?

As a married man who has watched lots of people "fall in love" (I put this in quotes because I think it's a poor description of what happens) and get married, and as a person who has counseled many couples before marriage and after marriage, let me give you some specific steps/suggestions in making this important decision. I think it's the second most important decision you'll ever make — second only to whether or not to accept Jesus Christ as your Lord and Savior.

Step One: *Realize men and women need each other.* Gladys

Hunt tells us, "Men and women need each other to fully appreciate what it means to be human.... One (male or female) without the other is incomplete humanity. We need the insights, the outlook, the expression of each other. That's why God puts us in families. He lets us observe the possibilities of maleness and femaleness in personal expression. We don't have to be married to appreciate this."

Gladys is not saying we all *have* to get married. Not everyone who is reading this book will get married. But married or not, we need each other to be fully human. Men need women. Women need men. Most of us will proba-bly want to get married. The Bible gives the suggestion that marriage is the norm for most people.

Step Two: *Ask yourself the question, am I ready to get married?* My friend, Steve Hayner, who is a leader in the Engaged Encounter movement says this, "It's more important to *be* the right person than it is to *find* the right person." Will you make a good mate? That's the question.

Several years ago, I devised a course on marriage for a publish-ing company. Included was a little checklist to help students better understand their readiness for marriage. Why not take a few moments now to look it over? And in a year or two, look at it

Your daughter tells me you're loaded . . .

again. Begin to work on the areas the survey addresses. For instance, if you don't love yourself you're going to have a hard time loving someone else. Self-esteem is important. Being responsible financially and being able to handle conflict are also important. Talk to God about the areas you feel you're weak. Read some books, talk to more mature leaders.

Prepare yourself in those areas.

Step Three: *Do you know what you're looking for?* God can, and sometimes does, surprise you with a person who has qualities you hadn't considered. And we will need to be flexible in what we look for in a mate. But it's important to do some thinking about what qualities you admire in a potential life partner. I have a

Relationship Readiness Self-Test

Are you ready for a serious, committed relationship? Answer each question by circling one of the numbers following it. A seven means "Yes, I pass that test." A one means "No, I don't measure up." This test is strictly personal.

1. I accept myself as a worthwhile person.

1   2   3   4   5   6   7

2. I have good friendships and can relate well with persons of my own sex.

1   2   3   4   5   6   7

3. I demonstrate unselfishness in my basic friendships. I'm able to be consistently concerned for the well-being of another person.

1   2   3   4   5   6   7

4. I have done everything possible to have a good relationship with my parents as adults.

1   2   3   4   5   6   7

5. I have a sense of responsibility and sacrifice to build a relationship that has higher goals than meeting my own needs.

1   2   3   4   5   6   7

6. I know how to handle conflict and frustration.

1   2   3   4   5   6   7

7. I am responsible in financial matters.

1   2   3   4   5   6   7

How well do you think a person should rate before he or she gets married?
After taking this test, would you now say that you are ready for marriage?

friend who has three qualities on her list. Because she has had a bad experience in a relationship with an alcoholic, her list looks like this: (1) the person must be a Christian, (2) he must not drink and, (3) he must look fairly good; not a hunk who models for GQ but a decent-looking individual. That's a fairly basic list. Only three items. Now a guy I know has this list of qualities he looks for in a woman: (1) she must love God, (2) she must be willing to be a partner in ministry and have skills in that area (he happens to be a guy who works with high-school and college students), (3) she must love and participate in athletics. That's it. He says nothing about body shape, looks, age, or hair color.

In that same marriage curriculum, a flexibility factor checklist was included to help determine the qualities that are most important in the person you marry. You might take a look at it too. I trust you'll place the highest value (5) in the blank next to marrying a Christian. In Scripture God says we are not to be unequally yoked together, and he's specifically talking about marriage. Again, I'd suggest you fill out the rest of this form now, and then come back and revise it as the years go by.

Step Four: *Are you dating?* How do you expect to marry in

Flexibility Factor Checklist

Everyone has some expectations his or her marriage partner must meet. Obviously some of these standards are more important than others. On a 1 to 5 scale, rate how you see the importance of each of these items. A five means that it's absolutely necessary to you that your mate qualify in this area. A one means you don't care. In between are degrees of negotiability. (If you have all fives, you're either a deluded dreamer or a confirmed celibate.)

How important is it to you that your mate:

☐ is a Christian ☐ is a mature Christian ☐ is a member of your denomination ☐ is a high-school graduate ☐ likes the same kind of food ☐ has good table manners ☐ agrees with you about sex ☐ gets along well with your family ☐ agrees with you about having children ☐ agrees with you about your respective roles in the home ☐ is comfortable with your friends ☐ is a good host or hostess ☐ laughs at the same jokes you do ☐ is punctual ☐ agrees with you about buying on credit or paying with cash ☐ lets you watch Monday night football ☐ knows how to resolve conflicts between you ☐ is in a habit of tithing ☐ agrees with you about revealing your pasts ☐ is articulate ☐ is physically attractive ☐ is an orderly person ☐ is a thinker ☐ is outgoing ☐ can cook ☐ has proven he or she can hold a job ☐ would be a good mother or father ☐ is respected by others ☐ consistently brings out the best in you ☐ is a virgin

Dating is valuable in three ways. (1) It helps you in your ability to communicate with a member of the opposite sex. This is important since in marriage you will *need to communicate*, and you *will be living* with a member of the opposite sex! (2) Dating provides you with the opportunity for social and cultural interaction, and (3) as you date you will test and learn social skills and realize your likes and dislikes, while discovering your own attractiveness. You'll find that someone besides your mother actually likes you!

Again, I say to guys, "Date!" A lot of Christian women resort to dating non-Christian guys because their Christian male friends simply don't date. While I don't feel there is anything wrong with associating with non-Christians and developing meaningful relationships, the obvious danger in dating non-Christians is that you might fall in love. Breaking up is so difficult, but breaking up is what would eventually have to happen if you desired to be obedient to God. It's a tough truth — God's will that we not become "unequally yoked." But it's God's will, nevertheless.

In a recent survey we did with our college students, we discovered that both men and women are afraid of rejection. But the men students seem particularly

this culture if you don't date? One of my pet peeves is Christian guys who don't date. They seem to think God will drop a girl on their doorstep someday with a note, "Hey, big fella, this one's for you. Handle with care. Get married in three days." God doesn't drop spouses out of the sky, and in our culture, parents don't arrange marriages. You arrange your own. Dating provides you with an opportunity to develop social skills and to get to know a variety of people. If you're not dating, you're not in a position to marry. I'm not suggesting you go out every night of the week. And I'm not against group dating. Group dating is fine but eventually you need to get to know people as individuals.

Telling a person "I love you" too soon can cause real problems.

fearful of rejection. To young women not being asked for dates, let me suggest that in "group dating" situations, you try bringing some guys around who might be feeling a little lack of confidence. They can get to know you and feel more comfortable around you. And both men and women should keep in mind, whether new to the dating game or when dating someone for the first time, that everyone is nervous in a dating situation. He's nervous. She's nervous. So be gracious to the other person and be gracious to yourself. Take a deep breath and be yourself.

And I would also suggest to both men and women that you bring the situation to God in prayer and then trust him. Whether or not you are dating, continue to live life fully, doing fun things with friends, and trust God with that area of your life. That may sound like a simplistic answer, but I know that God cares very deeply about you finding a suitable life partner.

Step Five: *Are you conducting yourself with integrity in the dating situation?* In other words, are you behaving yourself? People can be rushed toward marriage with the wrong people by their behavior on a date. Watch the physical contact, and be careful of what you say. Telling a person "I love you" too soon can cause real problems.

Step Six: *Are you infatuated or in love?* Unfortunately, God doesn't usually supernaturally

First the good news.
Both girls waiting for you
in the lobby, expecting a meal
and a movie, are beautiful. . . .

115

14 KEY CLUES TO DISTINGUISH INFATUATION AND LOVE

CLUES	CHARACTERISTICS	
1. What is your main interest? What attracts you most?	Person's "physical equipment;" the body; what responds to the five senses.	The total personality; whole person; what's *in* the body.
2. How many things attract you?	Few, though some may be strong.	Many or most.
3. How did the romance start?	Fast (hours or days)	Slowly (months or years).
4. How consistent is your level of interest?	Interest varies, comes and goes; many peaks and valleys; not consistent or predictable.	Evens out; gets to be dependable, consistent; can predict it.
5. What effect does the romance have on your personality?	Disorganizing, destructive; you act strangely, are not "yourself."	Organizing, constructive; you're a better person.
6. How does it end?	Fast, unless there's been mutually satisfying sex.	Slowly; takes long time; you may never be quite the same.
7. How do you view each other?	You live in a one-person world. You see the other as faultless, idealizing him or her.	You add the new relationship to former ones. You are more realistic, admitting other's faults, but loving anyway.
8. How do others view you two? What's the attitude of friends and parents?	Few or none approve of the relationship.	Most or all approve. You get along well with each other's friends and parents.
9. What does distance do to the relationship	Withers away, dies; can't stand this added stress.	Survives; may even grow.
10. How do quarrels affect the romance?	They get more frequent, more severe.	They grow less frequent, less severe.
11. How do you feel about and refer to your relationship?	Much use of I/me/my; he/him/his; she/her/hers; little feeling of oneness.	Speak of we/us/our; feel and think as a unit, a pair; togetherness.
12. What's your ego response to the other?	Mainly selfish, restrictive; "What does this do for me?"	Mainly unselfish, releasing; concerned for other.
13. What's your overall attitude toward the other?	Attitude of taking; exploit and use the other.	Attitude of giving, sharing; want to serve other's needs, wants.
14. What is the nature of jealousy?	More frequent, more severe.	Less frequent, less severe.
TOTAL PATTERN OF THE CLUES:	**KID STUFF; PUPPY LOVE**	**THE REAL THING; TRUE LOVE**

Summary clue: In real love you love the person so much that you want them to be happy, even if you may not be allowed to share their happiness.

From *Sex, Love, or Infatuation* by Ray E. Short

116

intervene with lightning bolts or stars in our eyes to let us know, "This is the one." You gradually come to know someone, and you begin to believe you'd love to spend the rest of your life with that person. But you need to be careful that your feelings are based on love, not infatuation. Dr. Ray Short, a sociologist, has spent much time considering the love/infatuation issue. Take a look at the chart he has developed, which is taken from his book, *Sex, Love, or Infatuation*. Study the clues he has provided to help you distinguish feelings of love from infatuation.

Step Seven: *Fish or cut bait.* You've been going with someone for a long time, you are in love, and that person meets most of the qualities you're looking for in a spouse. The next logical step is marriage. All systems are go for marriage. You are ready biologically. You are ready emotionally and psychologically. And you know that if you don't take the next step it's probably better to break up because the relationship will begin to disintegrate. Now seems the time to make a move. But obviously there must be balance in the situation. What if one of you still needs to finish school? And you will both want to hear your parents' wishes in this decision. After considering these

things, you might come to the realization that marriage will have to be postponed. You will then need to adjust the amount of time you spend together and the amount of affection you display.

In summary, you choose a mate with your *head* and your *heart*. You choose a mate in cooperation with God. That partnership between you and God is an exciting partnership; you trust him in the situation but you take the steps, you take the initiative to find that special someone in your life.

13

How to relate to your parents

When you graduated from high school your relationship with your parents changed. That relationship has been changing ever since you were born (and before that in the womb even) but it changes more drastically now. You are eighteen years of age. You are legally an adult. You are a high-school graduate. You are commencing. Moving on.

For eighteen years your parents have served several key roles in your life. They have been providers, nurturers, disciplinarians, directors. They have given you a shoulder to cry on. They've given you a pat on the back or a pat on the bottom, depending on what you've deserved.

As you've entered and moved through adolescence, your perceptions of your parents have changed. You recognize your father is not the most powerful man in the world. Your mom is not the smartest. In fact, they both seem to be less intelligent than you used to think they were. They do not seem to understand how the real world functions. They don't seem to know how to have fun. And they don't understand you. To paraphrase Mark Twain, "When I graduated from high school, my parents were the most foolish people on earth. I can't believe how much they matured in the four years I was away at college." So whatever your perceptions of your parents are now, expect those perceptions to change.

Graduation is such a momentous occasion in a parent-child relationship because it represents a new stage of life for both parties. Generally, parents are loosening their control and authority in your life. As you move into adulthood, what kind of relationship can you expect to have with your parents? What are some guidelines to keep in mind?

1. **Remember: Your parents have been adults for a long time.** They are probably more set in their ways than you are. They may not understand your need for adventure and risk, your desire for new and varied experiences. Be patient with them.

2. **At the same time, listen to them.** They know you well. For the most part, they have your best interest in mind. They've been around the block a few times. They have gained from their experience. Listen carefully. My wife likes to say that "parents may give you the right advice for the wrong reason." For instance, you might bring a friend home from school, and your parents may not like that friend. They don't recommend you develop that relationship. Their reasoning may be faulty (they might look at that person's external qualities, which aren't important to you) but their conclusion may be right. They have a hunch they can't express. Consider their hunches, even when their reasoning doesn't seem clear to you.

3. **God has created you. You are unique. No one else in the world is exactly like you. And God has given you your parents.** The Bible informs us of how God made us in our uniqueness, "For you created my inmost being; you knit me together in my mother's womb. I praise you because I am fearfully and wonderfully made" (Psalm 139). God knows you intimately, and he knew who your parents would be before you were born. (Or before they were born for that matter.) He allowed you to have the parents you have. Look to him to show you why you have the parents you have. What does he want to teach you about life from them? Even as an adult, what can you learn from them?

4. **Your parents are going to take a longer time to adjust to your newfound autonomy and freedom than you probably will.** In the midst of all the changes taking place in your life, it is very important you communicate with them. They want and need to know what's happening in your life. For many years they have played a significant role in your development, and for the most part, they have determined the direction your life has taken. Make them as much a part of your life as you can.

5. **The transition from your being a dependent child to being an independent adult is bound to produce some ten-**

sion. Tension brings out a person's strengths and their weaknesses. Try to put yourself in your parent's place as you work through this sometimes difficult time. Philippians 2:3,4 offers helpful advice: "Do nothing out of selfish ambition or vain conceit, but in humility consider others better than yourselves. Each of you should look not only to your own interests, but also to the interests of others."

6. **If you want your parents to change, be open to change yourself.** The last few years may have been turbulent at your house. Teenage years are sometimes rough on everybody. Mistrust may have developed between you and your parents. And there may be some hurt feelings. Your parents are hoping you'll change probably as much as you're hoping they will. So be open to examining areas where you might change or be more flexible.

7. **Parents are not your servants.** Nor are they a special source of funding or an insurance policy. When you become an adult, you can no longer expect your parents to provide in the way they've provided in the past. That's part of the deal. Your freedom means more responsibility on your part, and less on theirs. Don't expect them to bail you out.

8. **Take your parents off the pedestal.** They are not perfect, as you may well already know. But keep in mind that parents are

people. They have needs just as you do. They have their positive attributes, and their negative. As we all do. As you become an adult, you begin to see your parents as equals; you see them in a more balanced light. You see their mistakes. You understand their hurts. And you recognize that, like yourself, they need someone to listen to them, they need to hear they are loved. And like all of us, they have a hard time admitting their mistakes.

9. **Let your parents know you love them and appreciate them by your words and actions.** Thank them. Do something special for them. Occasionally bring home some goodies. Wash their car, even if they don't ask you to do so. Take an interest in them; ask about their work or their golf game. Surprise them with your gratitude.

10. **Remember the commandment from Deuteronomy 5:16,** "Honor your father and mother, as the Lord your God has commanded you, so that you may live long and that it may go well with you in the land the Lord your God is giving you." To honor means to prize highly, to care for, to show deep respect for. As you move into the age where you no longer have to obey your parents, you still need to honor them. Think specifically how you might do that.

11. **Remember that as an adult you are free to make decisions independently from your parents.** Sometimes, even though you

are not specifically doing what your parents say, you'll find yourself still trying to win their approval or please them. Bear in mind that God wants you to develop the unique skills he has given you. He wants you to seek his will rather than doing what you think will please your parents.

12. **For those of you who have been hurt by your parents, you will need to forgive them.** This is sometimes a painful and slow process. But it is absolutely necessary *for you*. It may be helpful to reread Chapter Seven, "Forgiveness as a Way of Life," and begin putting into practice forgiveness. Only by giving up hurts and angers can you really begin to grow up emotionally and spiritually. This may also require giving up the desire that your parents change to provide you what you missed growing up. It means moving on, not expecting your parents to make major decisions for you anymore. It means giving your primary allegiance now to God.

13. **Call home.** It's easy when you get away from home to lose touch with your parents. Call them. Write them. When you get a letter from home, read it carefully. What can you learn about them? And what can you learn from them? Remember, this is a relationship for a lifetime.

The change in the relationship with your parents is a big one. But it's worth the effort to make it a positive transition. Give it your best. Don't run away from the relationship, but don't feel trapped by it either.

Interestingly, as I was writing this chapter I learned something about my own relationship with my parents. I've always been very positive about my parents. But I realized that as an adult, I have not communicated with them as well as I should. I have not listened to them as well as I could. I have not asked them to talk to me about their needs, their concerns, what's happening in their lives. I have treated them as "my folks," and they are my kids' "grandpa and grandma," but I have not worked at knowing them as adults. I hope by the time you read this, I will have done a better job. I wish the best for you, too, as you relate as adults to your parents.

G. Keith Olson

Risking the ever-present possibility I am deluding myself, I'm pretty happy with the choices I made in my post-high-school years. There isn't much of a sense of pride in that statement because during that time and many times since, I'm convinced God spared me from my own great potential to make poor choices.

But here are a few things that I feel really good about.

• Though not understanding much about how God's will was supposed to work in my life, I was genuinely concerned that he would be influencing and directing me into my future. Though I accepted responsibility for making my own decisions, I felt a strong dependence on God for guidance during and after college.

• I was a serious student. I bought the party line that grades were important, so I studied hard to get them. "Delayed gratification" may not be such a popular idea but it worked for me.

• Psychology proved to be a good major for me in college. Chalk one up for God's leading.

• One of the smartest decisions I made during college was going to a professional counselor for help. I needed it! It was a scary step to take ... but it was worth it. By the way, he wasn't even a Christian therapist.

• I didn't get married until after completing my undergraduate program. No great wisdom on my part ... just too immature and scared to make that kind of commitment any earlier. I got a nose bleed when I finally did make that decision!

Well, those are the things I'm most happy about. Now for some of the things I'd like to have another turn at.

• Taking some basic accounting classes might have helped me to feel and be more competent at an earlier age in handling financial matters.

• A major "re-do" I'd make in my post-high-school years would be to approach my parents with a far more forgiving and accepting attitude. Critical attitudes and conflicts are a normal part of adolescence but I wish I could have resolved them sooner with my parents.

• I lacked the courage to get acquainted with and date girls during my first two years of college. I rationalized my insecurity by hiding behind my Christianity: "I can't go to dances," or "it's okay to only date the really spiritual girls," and "if I date a non-Christian it might ruin my life." While there may be valid concerns in these issues, religious paranoia mixed with my insecurity produced one very inhibited college freshman.

One last item. Now that I am into my forties, I'm finally beginning to really feel like an adult. Life is smoothing out, and inside I'm feeling more confident and competent. Adolescence and early adulthood are exciting. But those years can be scary and challenging too. It's a good feeling now not to always feel like I've got to prove myself to someone.

Dr. Keith Olson graduated from Grossmont Union High School in La Mesa, California, San Diego State University, and the University of Arizona where he earned his Ph.D. in Counseling Psychology. At the end of his Ph.D. program, Keith began working for San Diego Youth for Christ, establishing a counseling center and training YFC staff in counseling skills on local, state, and national levels.

He is currently providing professional psychotherapy services, writing books, doing video tapes and speaking on issues related to counseling adolescents, marriage, and family relationships.

PART FOUR

THE ROAD AHEAD

14

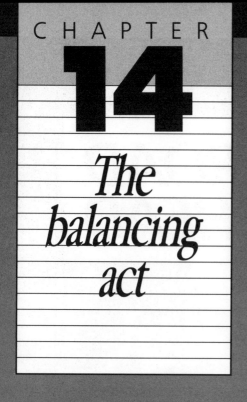

The balancing act

I have a complicated life with many opportunities and many demands.

I'm a husband. Married to a wonderful woman. And I have responsibilities (and benefits!) that come with the privilege of being married.

I'm a Dad. Four children. Two in junior high, one in kindergarten, and one preschooler. Their demands are varied and that makes my life complex. There's basketball, scouts, church groups, soccer, and band concerts with the two older kids and all kinds of different activities with the two younger ones.

I'm also a pastor. A director of University Ministries. I work with hundreds of college students each week. I love my job and wouldn't change it for the world, but it is demanding. I spend many hours with students and also have a full-time staff of ten people working with me. I want to do all I can to help my staff and our students be all they can be.

In addition, my wife and I have a ministry to members of the LPGA — the Ladies Professional Golf Association. We spend some time each year on the tour.

I'm also a friend. A neighbor. A writer. A reader. A member of an extended family (folks, grandmother, in-laws, and so on). I'm also a sometime athlete who enjoys playing tennis, racquetball, and basketball, and I'm on a softball team with a bunch of younger guys. I like that. I want to do a lot, to be a lot. I want to live a balanced life. I don't want to become a fanatic who is tied to work or consumed by my ministry.

Your life is probably busy too. Demanding. Complex. You've had to juggle a lot of balls and perform a balancing act in high school with your involvement in school activities, your studies, church functions, relationships, and parental demands. In the last few years, you've been a child, a friend, a student. Maybe you've even been a cook at McDonald's, an officer in your youth group, a tennis player, a brother or sister, and more.

I've got some hard news for you. The pace of your life and demands of your time accelerate during your college and adult years. Life doesn't slow down. Life doesn't become less complicated. And it doesn't get any easier. As writer Elisabeth Elliot says, "Life isn't tidy." It's tough to determine your priorities and find a balance you can live with in the midst of a busy life. But you can do it. The purpose of this book has been to help prepare you for the long haul, to give you the resources to live life to the max in college and

beyond. Which is why I want now to share a few more suggestions that are specifically geared to this subject of balance.

Let's begin with *perspective*.

The first concept to grasp is this: *"You'll never have it together; you'll always be working at balanced living."* At times life's demands on you will make you feel "out of sync." You'll always seem to be struggling to get enough time for the important things in your life. How can you study, spend time with that person you really like, take care of your own physical and spiritual needs, as well as work?

Plan your day or someone else will plan it for you.

The second concept is: *"Don't let others set your pace."* I have a theory I call the Rydberg Theory of Fanatics. I believe the Lord only puts a few fanatics in each generation but they are usually the people who write the kinds of books and magazine articles that make us feel guilty for not living up to a certain standard. (I hope this book doesn't serve that function in your life!)

I read in a magazine once about a guy who got up at 5:00 every morning and prayed. The guy's life was apparently dramatically changed, as were the lives of the people for whom he prayed. This character was an inspiration to me. I was motivated to follow his example. I decided I too would pray one hour every day. (This was back when I used to let others set my pace.) It was a killer. I found myself falling asleep as I struggled through a prayer list. But I was determined I would pray during this hour, every day.

Shortly after this, I read in a book about how a person can read the entire Bible through in a year, and in yet another book, I read about the importance of in-depth Bible study. So I began spending an hour in prayer, plus an hour in Bible study, per day. I was also into keeping my body fit so I was on the road running five miles a day. And all this before breakfast!

Soon I found I couldn't keep up this pace. I became irritable, so totally and compulsively caught up was I in the big three —

prayer, Bible study, and running. I wanted to be all I could be. I thought this was the way to do it, but my life was out of balance. Eventually I adjusted my pace. God knew what was best for me. He didn't want me to burn myself out before breakfast. He and I adjusted that schedule.

You and the Lord need to work out your lifestyle together. He knows you intimately. He knows what you need. He knows in what area you need to be challenged and in what areas you need to rest. You are responsible primarily to him, not to authors or spiritual giants you might read about.

As we consider the balanced life, and by that, I mean a life that exhibits harmony and stability and integration, I'd like to share with you three of my favorite "balanced" quotes.

The first comes from Gordon Dahl. He says:

> Most middle-class Americans tend to worship their work, to work at their play, and to play at their worship. As a result, their meanings and values are distorted. Their relationships disintegrate faster than they can keep them in repair, and their lifestyles resemble a cast of characters in search of a plot.

What Gordon is saying to us is that our priorities are out of whack. And, consequently, our values are distorted and our relationships are in trouble.

Let's look at quote number two. David Augsberger says this: "You must be first a person, then a partner, then a parent, and last of all a professional, whatever your profession may be: plumber, painter, politician, or preacher."

David gives us an overview of priorities. The first priority, to be a person, means we need to take care of ourselves (see quote number three below) and love ourselves so we can love others. Then, if you choose to become married, your next priority is to your spouse. If you choose to have children, your next priority is to them. Finally, you approach your profession. Just because it is the last priority doesn't mean you do a poor job in your chosen line of work. But it does mean that relationships are more important.

Full-time religious work doesn't grant you an exemption. You still have priorities more important than your work.

But how does this relate to someone like you, who may not be married or have children? Relationships are still the most important priority. You are to love and care for yourself. You must be a friend. Then you are a professional, in your case, a student or worker.

But let's look to quote number three for further clarification.

Jesus said, "Love the Lord your God with all your heart and with all your soul and with all your strength and with all your mind and love your neighbor as yourself."

I appreciate Jesus' words. I appreciate him and how, as we work on the balancing act in our lives, he helps us to get our priorities in order — by teaching us to love God, love ourselves, and love others.

Now with those preliminary thoughts in mind, how do we go

about living a balanced life? Let me give you some practical suggestions.

1. **Manage your time.** In an earlier chapter, I warned that it's possible to become an obsessive-compulsive person when it comes to time management. Obviously, a balanced person isn't compulsive. Here are some key points to help you find the right balance.

• Think of time as extremely valuable. Don't waste it unless you choose to do so. A balanced person needs to utilize the time.

• Know your own *prime time* and *work smart,* not just hard and long. I discussed this in greater detail in chapter seven but the point is: do the most important and most meaningful items at the time when you're at your best, whether that is morning, afternoon, or late evening time.

• Establish priorities. Know what's most important for you in the long term and the short term.

• Make and take a specific plan of action each day. "Plan your day or someone else will plan it for you." Schedule how you will use your time but be open to any interruptions and changes God may bring your way.

2. **Consider your priorities.** I've thought about this in my own life, and I have a set of priorities clearly defined in my mind and on paper. I don't always follow

through on my priorities, but I try. They are:

• Number One. *To be a friend and follower of God.* That's my top priority. That's how Jesus said it should be, and that's how I want it to be. I live out this priority by having *daily Bible study* since this is one of the major ways God speaks to me. That's how I can know, love, and serve him better, and discover his will for my life. I also spend time in *prayer,* talking and listening to my good friend and Lord. My participation in a *small group* helps me maintain a balance in my relationship with

God. Iron sharpens iron and relationships keep us sharp. And I attempt to be obedient. *Obedience* is a test of my love, and I do love Jesus.

• Number Two. *To be a friend to myself.* Remember the priorities Jesus listed? Love God and then love your neighbor *as yourself.* If I'm going to love my neighbor, I need to love myself. How do I do that? I take care of myself physically through regular exercise, watching what I eat, and getting enough sleep. I take care of myself by staying mentally fit. I forgive myself when I fail. I try to encounter experiences that will broaden and stretch me (like the recent evangelistic trip to Mexico I

mentioned earlier.)

• Number Three. *To be a friend to Marilyn.* A husband. To "love her as Christ loved the church" (Ephesians 5) is my goal. One of my responsibilities is to see that she has the freedom to develop her gifts and that she is fulfilled.

• Closely aligned to this priority is Number Four — *to be a father to my four children.* This means that I think about what it means to be a husband and dad. And I devote time to these important roles. One thing Marilyn and I do is schedule a date one afternoon each week. And we plan weekends away. I try to have a special day with my children each month and family nights each week. I consciously and intentionally control our calendar so that we can be a family. I try to be a good listener. I try to be available.

• Other priorities. Extended family. Close friends. Work. I want to do well in these areas, too, but I know that the first four priorities come before anything else.

I urge you to make my first two priorities your first two priorities. I believe being a friend of God and being a friend to yourself is biblical. This is what God wants us to do. And if there's one thing I've learned in my life here on earth, it's this: God knows what he's doing. And he knows what's best for us.

Here are few final suggestions to live a healthy, integrated life.

1. Don't kill yourself trying to be balanced. Do your best in God's strength and relax.

2. Find a support group. A small group. Loving, committed Christian friends can help you keep a balanced perspective by praying for you, listening to you, and holding you accountable when you lose perspective and when your life gets out of sync.

3. Have some outlets for frustration. I like to do something physi-

Work at bringing order to your life. That messy room, those things undone are all elements that drain life and vitality from you.

cal. Run, chop wood, ride my exercise bike. I know of a woman, a senior in college, who, when frustrated, drives around in her car and screams (with the windows rolled up). Another person I know plays the piano,

and another goes for long walks.

4. Work at bringing order to your life. That messy room, those things undone are all elements that drain life and vitality from you.

5. Don't overextend your standard of living. In other words, don't live beyond your means. Don't buy when you should be saving. Don't get over your head financially. Worrying about money and bills causes us to lose our perspective and balance.

6. Learn to say no. You can't do everything. You can't say yes to every need you see; you'll spread yourself too thin. Practice saying no. I wouldn't have a date with Marilyn every Wednesday afternoon if I couldn't say no to the other demands on Wednesday afternoons.

7. Pick a few daisies. Gary Warner, a friend of mine, found the following quote on a bulletin board several years ago. They are helpful words when it comes to finding a balanced life in a sometimes hectic world.

If I had my life to live over again, I'd try to make more mistakes next time. I would relax. I would limber up. I would be sillier than I have been this trip. I know of very few things I would take seriously. I would take more trips. I would climb more mountains, swim more rivers and watch more sunsets. I would do more walking and looking. I would eat more ice cream and less beans. I would have more actual troubles and fewer imaginary ones. You see, I am one of those people who lives prophylactically and sensibly and sanely hour after hour, day after day. Oh, I've had my moments and if I had it to do over again, I'd have more of them. In fact, I'd try to have nothing else. Just moments, one after another, instead of living so many years ahead each day. I have been one of those people who never go anywhere without a thermometer, a hot water bottle, a gargle, a raincoat, aspirin, and a parachute. If I had it to do over again, I would go places, do things, and travel lighter than I have.

If I had my life to live over, I would start bare-footed earlier in the spring and stay that way later in the fall. I would play hooky more. I wouldn't make good grades except by accident. I would ride on more merry-go-rounds. I'd pick more daisies.

— Brother Jeremiah

Now if you were a sloth who didn't much care about anything and who didn't work much, I probably wouldn't have included this quote from Brother J. But my hunch is you are hard working and very sincere about using your time well and making a contribution. I would encourage you in the pursuit of these wholesome desires to take time to pick some daisies too.

Here's to the balancing act. Here's to healthy living.

Phil Harmon

The late teens and early twenties are unique years — an exciting time of laying a foundation to build on for the rest of your life. I'm so glad that early on I had the opportunity to commit my life to God and to seek his guidance in preparation for a life full of challenges and opportunities.

I once heard someone in college say that "the kind of person you will be in five years will depend on two things: (1) the books you read, and (2) the people you associate with." That statement made a marked impression on my life. I decided to be bold enough to invite people I respected to be my guests for breakfast or lunch so that I could ask them some questions (that I had prepared in advance) about their philosophy. I was exposed to some really great people whose perspectives helped me form my own values.

One such individual was Dr. Ted Engstrom, president of World Vision. His gracious acceptance and affirmation of me has been a highlight of my spiritual pilgrimage and my development as a "whole" person.

If I had the opportunity to "do it over," I would certainly put more emphasis on study habits and apply myself more diligently in studying.

Philip E. Harmon is president of Harmon and Associates, a real estate, insurance and investment company. He graduated from Stadium High School (Tacoma, Washington) and attended George Fox College, the University of Washington and Seattle University. Phil has four children and ten grandchildren.

I would look for a more well-rounded curriculum to prepare me for life in general, not just my specific chosen field. I would have been better prepared for the challenges ahead if I had had an understanding of business and accounting, and if I'd acquired a solid grasp, not just of biblical principles, but of history. I also wish I had taken more academic courses dealing with human behavior.

Observing the lives of people who have overcome adversity, I have noted how they have established goals and sought with all their efforts to achieve them. From the moment you decide to concentrate all your energies on a specific objective, you are able to overcome the most difficult odds. You will also find that as you stretch your mind with new ideas or goals, it will never retreat to its original dimension.

I would get more excited about opportunities, remembering that it is "excitement that causes us to stretch, and stretching that causes us to grow."

Stretch yourself by being involved in student government, working on outside jobs, participating in intramural or intrascholastic athletic events. You'll be amazed at your potential! I've often been encouraged by the words of Charles Kettering, "You will never stub your toe standing still; the faster you go and the more you are involved in, the more chance for stubbing your toe, but the more chance you have for getting somewhere."

I'd be less afraid of failure. It's by failure that we learn and profit! Persistence, too, is a great instructor.

I used to sell cookware while in college. The lessons I learned on that job were every bit as important as my classroom education in preparing me for the realities of life. Making "cold calls," that is, knocking on strange doors in strange neighborhoods, taught me much in the way of human relations, self-confidence, and persistence.

President Coolidge had this to say about persistence, "Press on: nothing in the world can take the place of persistence. Talent will not: nothing is more common than unsuccessful men with talent. Genius will not; unrecorded genius is almost a proverb. Education will not; the world is full of educated derelicts. Persistence and determination alone are overwhelmingly powerful."

15

The long haul

L ife is a marathon, not a sprint.

I believe that. And you and I are to run this marathon; we're in it for the long haul. As a recent high-school graduate, you have on the average fifty-five more years of life left to live, if the Lord does not return and if you live out your normal span of life. That's a significant amount of time. That's approximately 482,000 hours of living.

This time is not to be taken for granted. You never know how long you will live. There are no guarantees. God wants us to redeem the time, to make the most of the fifty-five year, 482,000 hour span we have, or may not have.

And we are to run this marathon, this race, with integrity, with enthusiasm, and with God.

Hebrews 12:1-3 describes this race.

Therefore, since we are surrounded by such a great cloud of witnesses, let us throw off everything that hinders and the sin that so easily entangles, and let us run with perseverance the race marked out for us. Let us fix our eyes on Jesus, the author and perfecter of our faith, who for the joy set before him endured the cross, scorning its shame, and sat down at the right hand of the throne of God.

Consider him who endured such opposition from sinful men, so that you will not grow weary and lose heart.

This race is the Christian life. It is the life of following and obeying Jesus. From this passage, you can tell it's a marathon and not a 100-meter dash. As with any race, you begin by signing up. You choose to run the race by God's strategy. To be part of his team means giving your life to him. It means, first, acknowledging you are sinful and separated from God and, therefore, can't know and experience his love and plan for your life. It means you recognize that God loves you and wants to have a personal relationship with you. It means that you know Jesus Christ is God's only provision for sin. It means that you know you must individually receive Jesus Christ as Savior and Lord. That when you receive Jesus Christ as Savior and Lord you can know and experience God's love and plan for your life. It means that once you've said yes to Christ, you've admitted your need, received forgiveness from your sins, and asked him to be in control of your life.

I trust you've done that. That you've committed your life to Christ and signed up for the race. If not, I encourage you to think about this most important of

relationships in the next few days. I urge you to invite Jesus to be Lord and Savior of your life.

If you've signed up for the race, then you're ready to run. Let's isolate what God says about the race and draw some conclusions to help us run the good race.

1. **Life is a race. There is a prize. God wants us to run seriously.** On a marathon course there are hills and valleys. Some races are run in heat and some in cold. But regardless of the weather and the course, a runner

runs. The Bible uses the theme of a race several times. In 1 Corinthians 9:24-27 Paul says, "Do you not know that in a race all the runners run, but only one gets the prize? Run in such a way as to get the prize. Everyone who competes in the games goes into strict training. They do it to get a crown that will not last; but we do it to get a crown that will last forever. Therefore, I do not run like a man running aimlessly; I do not fight like a man beating the air. No, I beat my body and make it my slave so that after I have preached to others, I myself will not be disqualified for the prize."

2. **We don't run alone**. Hebrews 12:1 tells us that "we are surrounded by such a great cloud of witnesses..." This great crowd probably means all previous believers who've finished the race — Moses, Noah, Abraham, Sarah, Isaac, Jacob, Joseph, Paul, Peter, Barnabas, even your great-grandmother (if she was a believer). All of them are in the stands cheering us on. I like that. When I played ball in high school and college, I always seemed to do better when there was a crowd. Their enthusiasm lifted me up. That's what is happening in this race. Moses himself is cheering you on. What

a thought! It also means that the great cloud of witnesses knows when you're slacking off. With this crowd watching me, I want to give it my best shot.

3. **We need to prepare to run, and we need to stay in training.** Hebrews 12 tells us to get rid of those things that entangle and encumber us. Marathoners wearing rubber sweatsuits and weighted shoes would not only be laughed at, they would hurt their times and endanger their health. The Greek runners in the original Olympics ran naked to be unencumbered. (I'm not recommending you do that on your college campuses.) Their intense workouts, which began ten months ahead of competition, included a strict diet to shed any extra weight that would hamper their endurance. Ask yourself: *What is hindering me as I prepare to run?* It might be a specific sin, in which case you need to seek forgiveness

from God; you may need to build an accountability relationship with someone to help you stay away from that sin. (See Chapter Six on "Facing Temptation.") Perhaps it's guilt. Guilt can be resolved by receiving the forgiveness God offers us through Jesus Christ. Maybe it's bitterness that's holding you back. The antidote for bitterness is to extend forgiveness (see Chapter Seven). Perhaps it's a bad habit, the wrong circle of friends. Whatever it is, Christ tells us to shed it. He will help us. But we can't run entangled.

4. **Run to the end.** Sprinters are fortunate. They have assigned lanes and a visible target — the finish line. Distance runners have many more distractions along the way and must mentally discipline themselves to stay focused on their goal. Veteran distance runners check out a course in advance, noting the surface, terrain, and weather conditions. As Christians, we can't check out the entire course in advance. God only lets us live our life one day at a time. But he does tell us who to keep our eyes on — Jesus. And he tells us how to run a strong race. When I'm on a long training run, and I'm faced with a difficult obstacle (like a long, hard hill!), I concentrate on something just a few feet ahead of me. A rock, a tree, a mailbox. When I reach that

spot, I concentrate on something else only a few yards ahead. Before I know it, by concentrating on short-term objects, I've made the long run. We need to fix our eyes on Jesus. Running with our eyes on Jesus is especially important when we run on the dark and rainy days, the dark nights of the soul.

You are on the threshold of an exciting life. You have graduated from high school and have commenced on the rest of your journey. *Decide to run and win!*

My friends and I, who thought about this book and wrote it for you, want the best for you. We want you to be all God wants you to be, to experience all he has for you. And that is life abundant! Life

significant! Life incredible!

We have tried to give you some tools for the long haul. We've discussed you in this book, how incomparable and unconquerable you are. We've talked about perspective, about whether you want a title or a testimony. We've discussed the importance of taking risks and how you can do that. We've gotten specific about how you can make decisions, how to face temptation, how to practice forgiveness, and how to communicate with God. We've looked at some practical skills, like time management and study tips. We've considered how best to make choices in the areas of career and a life partner. We've talked about how, as adults, to relate to parents. We've discussed balance.

But ultimately, it's up to you to make your life what you want it to be, in partnership with God. If I could emphasize one thing, it would be that point. You are in partnership with Jesus Christ. Your life is not your own. He bought it with his life on the cross. But Jesus is not a ruthless master, rather he's wise and benevolent. He died for you so you could live life in a special dimension.

When I was a freshman in college, I wanted to always remember that fact. So I did something I think some upperclassmen found rather immature. I attached to the ceiling of my room, directly above my pillow, a sign. I took an old basketball shoestring and taped it to the ceiling, and hanging from it was a 3 x 5 card that said, "Christ Always Number One." I placed it so that immediately upon waking, I would sit up and bump into the card. A reminder. At the end of the year, a junior approached me about that card. "I saw you put that card up when you moved in here. I thought it was a stupid thing to do," he told me. "I also thought I'd watch you to see what difference it made. I concluded it made a difference. I've decided to put Christ number one in my life too."

I was excited about what this fellow told me. But you know what? The next year I decided I didn't need the card. It seemed a little beneath my dignity. And there were times over the years when I did not, in fact, make Christ Number One in my life. Times when I didn't live for Christ. I lived only for myself, and my life suffered as a result.

So I encourage you as you prepare for the marathon: Make Christ Number One and enjoy the next 482,000 hours making a difference in this world for him!

Beyond Graduation – Photo Credits